DATE DUE

IMPERIAL TEXAS

An Interpretive Essay in Cultural Geography

IMPERIAL TEXAS

An Interpretive Essay in Cultural Geography

By D. W. Meinig

Introduction by Lorrin Kennamer

UNIVERSITY OF TEXAS PRESS

AUSTIN AND LONDON

F
386
M35

Standard Book Number 292–78381–7
Library of Congress Catalog Card No. 69–18807
Copyright © 1969 D. W. Meinig

Type set by G&S Typesetters, Austin
Printed by The Steck Company, Austin
Bound by Universal Bookbindery, Inc., San Antonio

To
Aubrey, Campbell, and Stan
who have given me
my most pleasant
ties with
Texas

The Pacific alone will bound the mighty march of our race and our empire.

—Sam Houston, President
Valedictory to the Texas Congress, December 9, 1844

* * *

Texas is an empire in itself. It should be the aim of every parent and teacher to cultivate a State pride in the children.

—E. H. Cushing
The New Texas Primary Reader, 1863

* * *

It is quite the fashion in Texas to speak of "our imperial commonwealth."

—H. Y. Benedict and John A. Lomax
The Book of Texas, 1916

* * *

[Texas] is beginning to seep over the edges; Oklahoma, Arizona, New Mexico, even California, feel its mighty impact, and if we were writing about Europe instead of the United States, one might easily be tempted to a paragraph about Texas "imperialism."

—John Gunther
Inside U.S.A., 1947

* * *

I gather it must be very bothersome to feel that you are living in an empire when you are actually living in one-fiftieth part of a nation.

—Sean O'Faolain
"Texas," in *American Panorama*, 1958

PREFACE

Texans have long been taught to think of their homeland as an "empire" and to use that word as something more than just a grandiose name for a large area. Despite the natural tendency of other Americans to dismiss it as an irritating if harmless pretension, the Texan claim is substantial and their use of the term more than metaphorical. For, leaving aside the common political connotation, if "empire" implies not only a relative size, but a history of conquest, expansion, and dominion over a varied realm, and not only an outward movement of people, but the thrust of a self-confident aggressive people driven by a strong sense of superiority and destiny, then Texans can reasonably claim a strongly "imperial" history and character.

However, although I have titled this essay and couched it in such a context, it is the general concept and not the terminology that is important. My principal concern is not to argue for "empire" but to look at Texas in a particular way. Basically I have traced its development (development not of the state as a political unit, but of the area as a human region) from an early simple framework and nucleus to the complexities of its present patterns with a view toward assessing the degree to which it evolved as a distinctive culture area and an autonomous functional region. This has led, on the one hand, to an emphasis upon the various peoples of Texas, who they are, where they came from, where they settled, and how they are proportioned one to another from place to place; and, on the other, to an emphasis upon strategies of territorial organization, how areas have been brought into focus, connected one to another, and bound up into larger networks of circulation. Applying this dual concern for regional patterns of culture and for regional systems of commerce to the successive layers of Texas history has resulted in a work which is superficially historical in structure but fundamentally geographical in character. So far as I am aware it has no parallel in the literature on Texas or any other American area and I hope that it will be received as a useful complement to more standard·views.

Certain premises and terms must be made clear at the outset. Underlying this entire essay is the assumption that race, language, religion, and national origin have always been and still remain important features in American life, features which have tended (however much we deplore the fact) to identify and separate people in fundamental ways. I have further accepted the idea that there are some deep-seated regional differences in values and patterns of behavior among the peoples of the different parts of the United States. I am well aware that there are great differences of opinion among sociologists as to how important these features really are and how they can be defined and measured; but this debate can never be fully resolved, and one simply must proceed on the basis of one's own judgment of the evidence as gathered from living as well as from studying. I can perhaps most easily make my position clear by citing two books —Milton Gordon, *Assimilation in American Life* (New York: Oxford University Press, 1964), and Richard E. Engler, Jr., *The Challenge of Diversity* (New York: Harper & Row, 1964)—as together defining very well the kinds of differences, their social significance, and their regional variability, which I have accepted as important.

I have used the term *culture* in its general anthropological sense, and *cultures* to refer to groups of people, each exhibiting in some significant way its own distinctive "configuration" or "way of life." Here again in an essay of this sort one has little choice but to accept certain generalizations and gloss over a welter of nagging difficulties. One difficulty which cannot be avoided is the need for simple labels for the several specific cultures discussed. Usually the term *Anglo* in this essay refers to the dominant people of Texas who are white, Protestant, Anglo-Saxon in ancestry, and Southern in heritage. At times, however, it should be obvious from the context that it has been broadened to refer to the general Anglo-American culture dominant over the whole nation. After considering the whole list of terms in use in the various parts of the Southwest I decided to follow the lead of many writers on New Mexico and to adopt the term *Hispano* as a simple, euphonious, and neutral name for the Spanish-speaking peoples whose ancestry is rooted in Mexico. Although in Texas such people are almost always referred to as Mexicans, there are of course many objections, technical and psychological, to such usage. *Negro* most obviously connotes race in America, but wherever such people are found in groups they certainly constitute a distinct sub-culture and are so considered here. I have used *European* to refer to those groups which came directly from Europe to Texas and maintained for some time a non-English-speaking society.

In referring to broad regions of America I have used *Upper South* and *Border South* as synonyms to designate the area extending from Virginia into Missouri, and *Lower South* and *Deep South* for that from South Carolina west through the Gulf states. The *East* refers to the Middle Atlantic-New England region; the *Middle West, Midwest,* and *Midlands,* all to that vague and general area from Ohio to the Great Plains focused upon Chicago and St. Louis. The *North* combines the *East* and *Middle West* into a single general region in apposition with the *South.*

Finally, I would like to emphasize that this is very much an exploratory essay and not a definitive analysis. Geographers, I think, run a particularly dangerous risk in such an endeavor simply because people have a strong tendency to accept maps as inherently definitive and as reliable sources of reference whereas they may be quite tentative and impressionistic. I am particularly concerned that my maps of culture areas and imperial gradations be accepted as no more than expressions of ideas and a stimulus to thought and not as definitive depictions of actual patterns. And of course one hopes as much for the entire essay: that it will be read as a geographer's contribution to the general and continual interest in what it is that makes Texas such a remarkable and singular place.

D. W. Meinig
Syracuse, New York

ACKNOWLEDGMENTS

The field reconnaissance and library research in Texas and the time for writing and the costs of preparing the text and maps for this study have been supported by generous grants from the John Simon Guggenheim Memorial Foundation and Syracuse University. All the original maps were based on my rough sketches, but were drafted in finished form by Miss Molly Debysingh, under the supervision of Mr. John Fonda, cartographer.

I wish to thank Dr. Llerena Friend for her help and interest which made research in the Eugene C. Barker Library of Texas History such a pleasant experience; and especially I wish to thank my good friend and host on three Texas visits, Dr. Stanley A. Arbingast, associate director of the Bureau of Business Research at The University of Texas, for many materials and suggestions, and, above all, for his most generous hospitality.

D.W.M.

CONTENTS

LIST OF ILLUSTRATIONS
(follows p. 96)

LIST OF MAPS

INTRODUCTION

The drama of Texas is more in the people than in the place. Yet, the full story must contain the elements of both. Texas is and has been a confluence of physical and cultural factors which have produced its uniqueness. The special interrelationship of peoples and place through time has made this a state of singular interest.

What are these factors which so focus upon Texas that the state can be called a meeting place? A look at the physical side shows great variety probing into the state from elsewhere in the continent. The eastern plains of the state are a continuation of the large Atlantic and Gulf Coastal Plain which extends from the Yucatan to Cape Cod. The North Central prairies and woodlands of the state come from the vast interior lowlands of the Midwest, while the High Plains are part of the great north-south High Plains of the continent's interior. In the western part of the state is the southern extension of the Rocky Mountains. Thus, the state serves as a place of focus for some of the continent's major landforms—plains, lowlands, plateaus, and mountains. And within these landforms are the many minerals which have played their role.

There is a confluence also of the continent's major vegetation patterns. The eastern part of the state receives the lush pine forests of the south, from the north come the belts of hardwood timber, while from the northwest there are the great short grasslands of the interior. Meanwhile, residing in southwestern Texas is true desert vegetation. To be expected, the major climatic groups come to focus in a similar pattern—humid subtropical climate from the southeast, humid continental from the north, and desert from the west.

Woven within this confluence of physical elements have been many cultures at different stages of time. The rich environmental variety has received the thrusts of different national and cultural backgrounds. These too have been rich in variety—Spanish, French, Mexican, Alsatian, German, Negro, English, Norwegian, Czech, and Polish. Out of all this, a state has been made.

We know, as observers of the scene today, that there are regional patterns within the state. Even if boundaries are not exact, we know there is an East Texas, a South Texas, and so on. These regions are not in existence because of a direct decision of a political legislature to create them: they exist of their own accord. Different cultures reacting with each other and with environments over a period of time have produced this regional pattern which makes up Texas. There has been something in addition that has welded these regions together in an even larger dream. The state is not just so many competing regions or counties but a whole cluster of subcultures held together with conscious effort, around symbols, dreams, and a sense of destiny.

To trace the origin and development of this sense of destiny (*i.e.*, the imperial dream of Texans) makes a most interesting and important study. What were the first signs of this dream? How have the present-day regions come to be and how are they related to the earliest regions of the state? What are the historical-geographical roots of current patterns of population, trade, and transportation? To answer these questions one must study the place, people, languages, origins, and religions; in other words, the human geography of the state.

The case is made accurately and in a most interesting way that, in regards to Texas, a state of mind has risen just as much as a physical state. There is more to Texas than the 254 counties, the resources, the people, and their activities. How did this come to be? Why did this come to be? This scholarly interpretive essay in the cultural geography of Texas by Professor Donald Meinig is a fascinating quest for answers to these questions and will be of interest to Texans and non-Texans alike.

LORRIN KENNAMER
Lubbock, Texas

IMPERIAL TEXAS

An Interpretive Essay in Cultural Geography

Chapter I

★ IMPLANTATION

~~~~~~

IF WE RECKON THE HISTORY OF TEXAS' DEVELOPMENT AS EX-
tending from the initiation of the first substantial missions
among the Tejas Indians in 1690 down to the present, the Spanish and Mexican portions of that history still constitute a little
more than half of the total span. Geographically, as by almost
any other measure, the results seem very small for so large a
proportion of time. But they were fundamental, even if simple:
a spare but lengthy framework of sites and routes, a small but
vigorous colonization nucleus, a thin but clear patterning of regional differences in people—the elemental matrix for all the
imperial dreams and designs that followed hard upon.

A SPANISH TEXAS

Spanish Texas was a remote and dangerous frontier, huge in
area, vague in definition, and, to the end, meager in development. In general it encompassed the country between the
Nueces and the Red River (later contracted slightly in the east
to the Sabine); and although it might appear from the considerable sprinkling of names and the network of trails on some of
the maps of its time as a great northeastern advance of Spanish
colonization, it was in fact more an area of widespread missionary failure and of a tenuous feeble thrust against foreign powers
in the lower Mississippi, and it had so little substance as to be
affronted almost at will by the Comanches on one side and

smugglers and filibusterers on the other. Yet it left an indelible
if highly localized imprint and its sparse geographic framework
helped shape the more substantial patterns which followed.

That framework became anchored upon three points: San
Antonio (de Bexar), Goliad (La Bahia), and Nacogdoches
(Map 2). The first was the oldest and long the main center—
initially a presidio with, soon, a town and several missions
nearby, and, eventually and in varying degrees, the administrative capital of the province. The second was essentially similar
in setting and elements though somewhat smaller in development and importance. These two were footholds on the southerly
margins of Texas, widely spaced along the San Antonio River,
on a strip of well-watered prairie and open brush country which
never failed to excite the admiration of Spanish travellers. Lying between the sandy plains beyond the Nueces and the broadening woodlands beyond the Guadalupe, it was considered an
ideal ranching area and it was in every way a land which the
Spanish could colonize in accordance with centuries-old rou-
tines. Missions, presidios, and pueblos were laid out in stand-
ardized patterns, lands in town and country were systematically
apportioned among the various ranks of settlers, a political hierarchy allocated irrigation water, imposed economic controls, and
maintained civil order. The early civil nucleus of San Antonio
was formed by a group recruited from the Canary Islands, but
most of the population, here as elsewhere on the frontier, was
recruited from the long-settled areas of central Mexico. Many of
the colonists at Goliad, for example, were a small part of a
much larger contingent gathered from Queretaro by a Spanish
empresario who founded Laredo and a score of settlements in
the lower Rio Grande Valley (then a part of the neighboring
province of Nuevo Santandar).

But Nacogdoches was a very different sort of place. It was
different because it lay deep in a very different kind of country
and over against a very troublesome frontier. The site was near
some of the earliest (but later abandoned) missions, but the
town was a late development following a succession of abortive
Spanish efforts. Its small garrison represented a retreat westward from the old presidio at Los Adaes founded sixty years

Map 1

The Terrain of Texas
(Reproduced by permission from Erwin Raisz, *Landforms
of the United States*, sixth revised edition, 1957.)

Map 1

The Terrain of Texas
(Reproduced by permission from Erwin Raisz, *Landforms
of the United States*, sixth revised edition, 1957.)

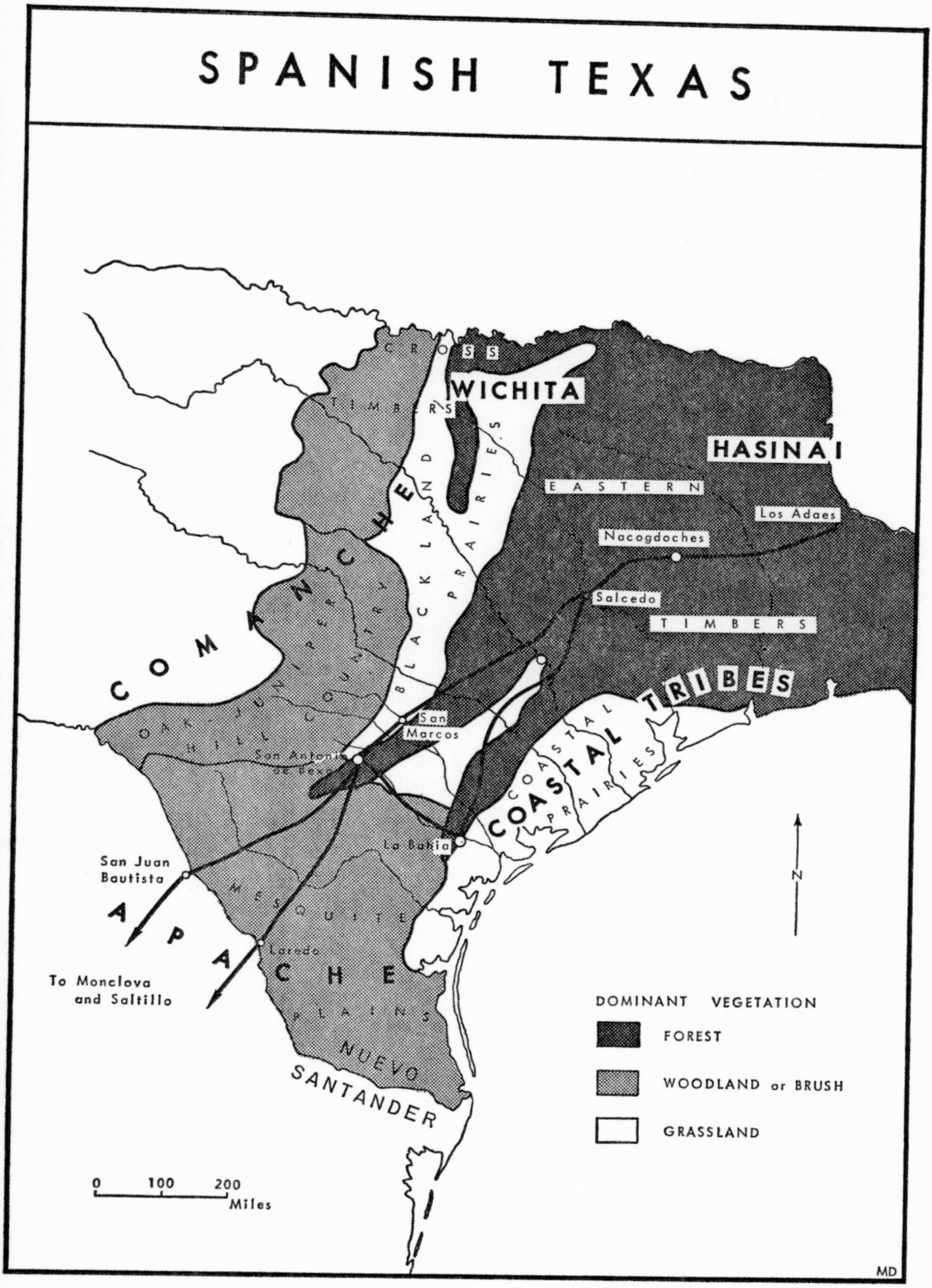

SPANISH TEXAS

COMANCHE

CROSS TIMBERS

WICHITA

BLACKLAND PRAIRIES

HASINAI

EASTERN

Los Adaes

Nacogdoches

Salcedo

TIMBERS

OAK JUNIPER COUNTRY

HILL COUNTRY

San Marcos

San Antonio de Bexar

COASTAL TRIBES

COASTAL PRAIRIES

San Juan Bautista

La Bahia

MESQUITE

N

A P A C H E

Laredo

PLAINS

NUEVO SANTANDER

To Monclova and Saltillo

DOMINANT VEGETATION

FOREST

WOODLAND or BRUSH

GRASSLAND

0   100   200
Miles

MD

Map 2

earlier on the edge of French Louisiana, while the town itself
represented a shift eastward from the brief settlement at the
crossing of the Trinity, which the officials had considered more
strategic. Much of this instability of the Spanish position stem-
med from a failure to attract the usual sort of Spanish colonists;
for Nacogdoches lay deep in the forests of East Texas, a hundred
miles beyond the nearest prairie openings. Clearly ranching in
the Spanish style was impossible; and the "long, endless thick
woods," full of swamps and insects, were repellant to travellers
from the high dry plateaus of Mexico. Thus, most of the population here had simply accrued rather than colonized under the
usual procedures, and it was a motley group of adventurers,
refugees, and drifters from many countries. The largest number
came from French (for a time, Spanish) Louisiana, but even
these were a heterogeneous lot. The chief attractions were freedom from homeland authorities and the profits and excitement
of illicit trade. And thus Nacogdoches was quite unlike the
typical Spanish colonial town of northern Mexico. It had a set
of officials but it was never formally designated as a pueblo or
a presidio, its social and civic life had little of the normal cohesion and stability, and the surrounding countryside was not
parcelled out among ranchers but was loosely occupied by a
scattering of squatters, Indian traders, and smugglers.

The trails connecting these three places formed the essential
areal framework of Spanish Texas. There were numerous attempts to enlarge it, by missionary work far into the hills of San
Saba, by garrisons and missions at various points near the Gulf;
but none of these succeeded, and only this lean tenuous triangu-
lar frame lasted through a century of Spanish rule. It was linked
to the main network of Mexico by a pair of long desert roads
from San Antonio to Monclova and Saltillo (the former long the
capital of Coahuila, and each the seat of various officials with
certain powers over Texas). That the main axis for all this era
should have run parallel with but well inland from the lengthy
Gulf coast rather than leading directly to one or more Texas
ports was a striking geographical expression of the rigidities of
Spanish policies. Foreign trade was tightly controlled and dis-
couraged: not even local traffiic along the Gulf was allowed, and

Veracruz was the only authorized port for Texas as it was for the rest of Mexico. Nacogdoches was the sole legal portal by land, and the fact that it fronted the only region of European settlement along the entire continental breadth of the Spanish borderlands was the reason for its being and the source of its character.

Clearly the outstanding internal geographical feature of Spanish Texas was its obvious division between two regions strikingly different in landscape and people, in purposes and problems: the one wholly a normal extension of Spanish colonization, distant and detached, but a logical step beyond the Rio Grande, bound by traffic and traditions entirely to Coahuila and the Mexico beyond; the other from the first a military and missionary effort, unable to attract the usual colonists, its heterogeneous population oriented toward Louisiana, drawing its sustenance directly from the troublesome conditions of an ill-defined border zone, with little firm allegiance to any authority.

Such a pattern presented Spanish strategists, who were chronically concerned about their weakness in this far corner, with two simple but difficult alternatives. The more conservative advocated withdrawal to the only part of Texas worth living in, holding to San Antonio-Goliad as not only a fine ranching country but a necessary shield for Coahuila and Nuevo Santandar against the incursion of the dreaded Comanches. However, others insisted upon the importance of retaining East Texas in order to stem the advance of foreign powers and to control immigration, trade, and contacts with the Indians. If properly managed, such an otherwise unwanted region could serve as a very useful buffer. But it was obvious to its advocates that the latter policy required a much more substantial presence, and in the early years of the nineteenth century some real efforts were made to provide it. Chief attention was directed to the need for colonies along the main axis, that long lonely road undulating broadly across the gentle grain of the country for more than three hundred miles between San Antonio and Nacogdoches. In 1805 settlements were authorized at each of the main river crossings. The two nearest the established towns, at the San Marcos on the west and at the Trinity (Salcedo) on the east,

were actually undertaken. Each was an offshoot of and typical
of its region: the former composed of a group of stockmen from
the San Antonio and Goliad areas, all natives of Texas or nearby
Mexican provinces; the latter a miscellany of farmers and traders from Louisiana, the United States, and a variety of European
nations. Neither colony survived the Indian raids and the generally chaotic conditions during the last decline of Spanish
power. In general Spain failed to colonize the timbered lands
of Central and East Texas simply because she did not want
the only colonists willing to come. Few Mexicans had any de-
sire to live in such a country, and the only people who did
were Louisianans and Anglo-Americans whom Spain feared
as politically unreliable. She finally did decide that a system-
atic recruitment of foreign colonists under very careful controls
was the only answer, but it was then so late that such a policy
could only be implemented not by Spain but by the new Republic of Mexico.

Thus after more than a century of effort the Spanish had
produced only this sparse structure of three settlements and
three or four thousand people. The really important geographical feature was that here in the deepest layer of Texas civiliza-
tion, there was already an important cultural regionalism: two
lands with very different peoples and very different interests.

B. Mexican Texas

The great feature of the Mexican regime was the vigorous
attempt to do just what the Spanish had failed to do: colonize
the broad middle zone, that great void between San Antonio
and Nacogdoches. Politically, of course, the great, ironic consequence was that in so doing Mexico greatly weakened rather
than strengthened its hold. At the same time, an obvious geographical consequence was the enlargement of the settled area
of Texas, and, less obvious but no less important, the modifica-
tion of its regional cultural character.

The decisive innovation was the Austin Colony, originally
authorized by the Spanish to Moses Austin and, after his death,
reconfirmed by Mexico and implemented by his son, Stephen
F. The first, the most famous, and by far the most successful of

the *empresario* grants under Mexico, it was central in area to and a model in plan for those granted thereafter. The system itself was a well established part of Spanish colonization. An *empresario* was one granted a large tract of country contingent upon its settlement by a specified minimum number of families; during the course of colonization he was an agent of the government accountable for the selection of colonists, allocation of lands, and imposition of all the various regulations pertaining to citizenship. The Austin grant was unusual only in that the *empresario* proposed to recruit his settlers from the United States. That was well understood at the time to be an important difference, but one which Mexico presumed to overcome by careful requirements imposed upon each colonist, as to civil and religious allegiance.

Austin was assigned a huge block of country embracing much of the lower Brazos and Colorado basins, bounded on the north by the old main road and on the south by a broad coastal strip from which, as from an even broader border strip to the east, Mexico, for the time being, wished to exclude foreign colonists (Map 3). It was a good location to meet Mexico's interests: central within the effective framework of Texas yet insulated a considerable distance from existing settlements and problem areas. And it was good country for the kinds of colonists Austin sought: broad bottomlands and gentle interfluves, a fine mixture of prairie and woodland, richly grassed and well-watered, a country to delight the eyes of any used to appraising the humid woodlands of eastern America. And not only was it an apparently bountiful land; it could be had in munificent amounts, for, true to Spanish traditions, it was offered in huge ranch-sized units—a square league (approximately 4,428 acres) to each family. And so even before Austin could lay out his capital town of San Felipe on a low bluff overlooking a good anchorage on the Brazos, the first landseekers arrived. Soon they were coming in from all the western frontiers of Anglo-America, from adjacent Louisiana and Arkansas, from Alabama, Tennessee, Kentucky, and Missouri, mostly overland—families, in many cases with their slaves (unwanted but tacitly allowed by Mexico), driving their cattle and hogs through

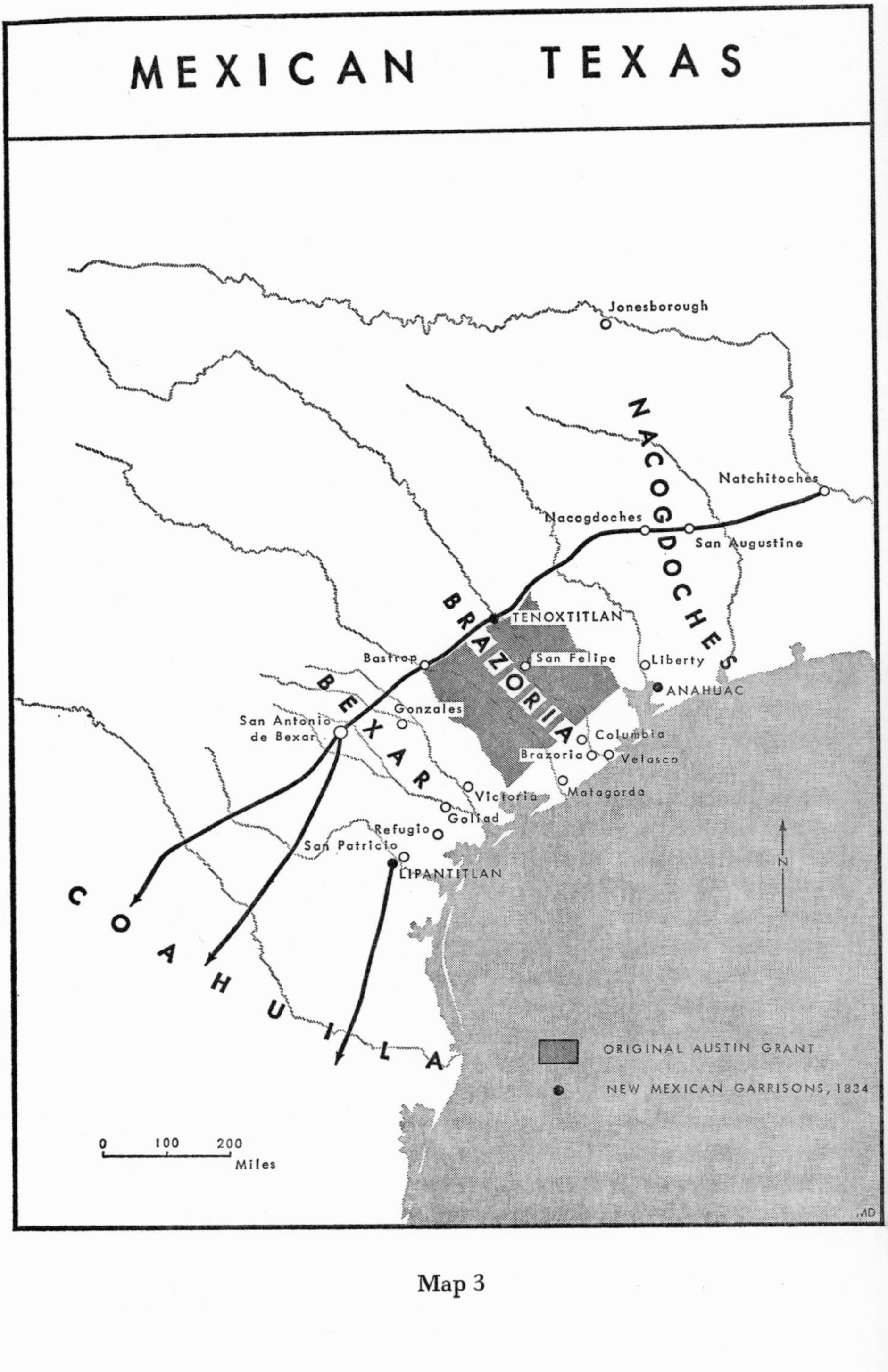

MEXICAN TEXAS

Jonesborough

NACOGDOCHES

Natchitoches

Nacogdoches

San Augustine

BRAZORIA

TENOXTITLAN

Bastrop

San Felipe

Liberty

ANAHUAC

Gonzales

San Antonio
de Bexar

BEXAR

Columbia

Brazoria

Velasco

Victoria

Matagorda

Goliad

Refugio

San Patricio

LIPANTITLAN

N

C O A H U I L A

ORIGINAL AUSTIN GRANT

NEW MEXICAN GARRISONS, 1834

0   100   200
Miles

Map 3

Nacogdoches and down the old La Bahia road to San Felipe to file for great riverine holdings. Austin eventually received some additional tracts, including the bordering coastal strip, and thus his colonists eventually filled in along the Brazos, Colorado, and lesser streams all the way from the old Camino Real to the Gulf.

In time lands on the three sides of Austin's colony, and some more distant, were granted to other *empresarios*, who varied greatly in their success in recruiting colonists and importantly in the kinds of colonists recruited (Map 4). Along the south-western side of the Austin Colony, DeWitt laid out his city of Gonzales on an elaborate plan and distributed nearly two hundred families, almost all Anglo-Americans, along the waters of the upper Guadalupe. Downstream, a Mexican, DeLeon, attracted by an area he had seen while driving mules to New Orleans, received a small grant wherein he established the town of Victoria and settled about forty Mexican families on the rich coastal prairies just east of Goliad. Farther south two sets of Irish *empresarios* contracted to introduce several hundred families, half of whom were to be Irish Catholics, the other half Mexican. Unfortunately many of the former died of cholera enroute or shortly after landing and few of the latter were attracted. San Patricio de Hibernia and Refugio, the capitals for these schemes, were laid out on the flat mesquite plains bordering Copano Bay and the lower Nueces, but for years each was central to only a small scattering of settlers.

To the north, above the San Antonio-Nacogdoches road, a few loose clusters of colonists were settled on the several grants. It was good country, but remote from the sea and dangerously exposed to Comanche raids from the west. In the last years of Mexican rule the broad border zone to the east was also apportioned and attracted a good many settlers, chiefly to the lower Trinity and the area around Galveston Bay.

The several *empresarios* issued a total of about thirty-five hundred titles to actual colonists and near the end of the Mexican period the population was at least twenty-five thousand, including slaves, and perhaps considerably more. Although that was not many people for so large an area, it was a remarkable

increase in so short a time, when compared with the century of
Spanish efforts. But it was an increase obtained only at a risk
the Spanish had been unwilling to take; for, despite special efforts to recruit Mexicans and Europeans, probably four-fifths
of the new colonists were Anglo-Americans. Mexican officials
had recurrent doubts about the wisdom of allowing such an
influx of aliens from a bordering nation into a border region.
They persistently refused to detach Texas as a separate state
from Coahuila, and they actually suspended such colonization
from 1830 to 1834, but this pause only caused a heavier surge
upon repeal.

It was during that interim that a strategic plan to strengthen
greatly the Mexican presence was initiated. Texas was divided
into three departments, and several new garrisons bearing prestigious Mexican-Indian names were established, each of which
was to be the focus of and was to be supported by a large body
of Mexican colonists (Map 3). As a result, each department had
a pair of forts, one along the old Spanish axis, the other on or
near the coast (Mexico had opened the Gulf to local trade); San
Antonio and Lipantitlan (and also Goliad) in the Department
of Bexar, Tenoxtitlan and Velasco in Brazoria, and Nacogdoches
and Anahuac in the Department of Nacogdoches. But although
such a strategy was sound in geography it was weak in per-
formance, for there were neither sufficient troops nor enough
colonists to make it effective. Thus when the gates were again
opened to American immigration the new Mexican settlements
in the two eastern departments were like foreign enclaves on
their own soil—tiny Hispano-American outposts caught in the
swirl of the Anglo-American frontier.

These three new political departments of 1834 were an accu-
rate if indirect reflection of new patterns in cultural geography.
The Department of Bexar remained the Hispanic region, in-
significantly diluted by the few Anglos or the Irish colonists
along the coast. Nearly two-thirds of the population was con-
gregated in and around San Antonio, still the principal seat
of Texas officials and the gateway between the Mexican nation
and its distant frontier. The remainder were too few even to be
spread thinly over the rest of the department, and they were

loosely clustered around Goliad and Victoria, San Patricio and
Refugio (an official inspection of 1834 found not a single ranch
between San Antonio and Goliad). But even such tiny primitive
centers were faithful if rather feeble exhibits of their common
heritage. They represented a civic-centered ranching culture
with all of the basic elements and character of the now long-
stabilized Mexican pattern: a cohesive, hierarchical structure
of Spanish, Mestizo, and Indian—Catholic and formal, authori-
tarian and conservative; a typical society of officials, soldiers
and priests, ranchers and foremen, vaqueros, carters, and peons.

The cultural contrast between the Departments of Bexar
and Nacogdoches was even greater than in the Spanish period.
Nacogdoches town in its plaza and neat straight streets and its
municipal organization continued to exhibit something of its
Spanish inheritance. But just as such forms had seemed alien in
appearance when set upon a red hill amidst the forests of East
Texas, so they were now even more alien in meaning to most of
the inhabitants of the town and the region. For the whole locale
was now strongly dominated by Anglo-Americans. Although
several hundred representatives of the earlier heterogeneous
population lived in and around the town, they were now so out-
numbered and most of them so firmly relegated to the bottom
of society (being regarded by Mexican officials and Anglos
alike as an ignorant shiftless group) that they exerted little influence upon developments in the area. The Anglo-American
newcomers were in some ways as motley a group as their pred-
ecessors, and many of them had been lured by the same attractions: the security and the opportunities of an ill-policed border
zone. The Mexican era coincided with a rapid increase in
American activity in the Mississippi Valley, and the political
boundary served increasingly as a selective social screen upon
the restless westward moving population of the American frontier, blocking the flow of those with strong attachments to the
institutions of their homeland and positively sucking in those
who had strong reasons to escape its laws. Certainly not all
who came were fleeing debts and courts, but the proportion
who were, together with the drifters and adventurers, the
smugglers and speculators, was very high. Thus Nacogdoches,

the new town of San Augustine (the very name a hybrid from the two languages), and the countryside around became strongly characterized by such people. And despite these two towns, which together had about six thousand people in their environs, there was no cohesive civic society. Indeed, it was the very antithesis of such a society that served as a main attraction of Texas. The local government land commissioner, who, typical of the region, was an Anglo-American, put it in the most pure and persuasive American frontier terms: "I am convinced that Texas must prosper. We pay no taxes, work no public roads, get our land at cost, and perform no public duties of any kind."

Such attractions had also lured Anglo-Americans into two other districts of this department, one far to the south, the other equally far to the north. Numerous squatters had settled at various points along the lower reaches of the Neches and the Trinity well before that area had been granted to *empresarios*. The efforts of the latter added a few more authorized colonists and a greater number of land speculators, especially in and around Liberty, which was expected to become a main shipping point for the region. Far to the north of Nacogdoches Anglo-Americans had begun probing the Red River Valley by about 1815, in a manner archetypical of the Upper South frontier movement of its time: exploration and transitory settlement by trappers and Indian traders, then the infiltration by a few families, each of which drove in a few hogs, built a cabin, and cleared a patch of ground, but lived as much by hunting as farming. Although such settlers were virtually cut off from the world of commerce, the links with family and friends in Arkansas, Tennessee, and Kentucky lured such a continual influx that by 1830 settlement began to spread beyond the Red River bottoms onto the rolling hills and small prairies to the south. The whole movement was entirely without formal direction. Indeed, so far removed was it from the arm of any administration that there was much uncertainty about what jurisdiction it fell under, and the area was first organized as a county of Arkansas Territory and so remained until 1836. However, Mexican officials always claimed the area, and the settlers, well aware of the ambiguity, sought confirmation of their land titles from both nations. Land litigation was probably the main reason for bothering to organize a county and to establish Jonesborough as its seat. The latter was a typical frontier cluster of rude cabins and taverns, even less expressive of civic society than Nacogdoches. In such frontiers the community was not focused upon a town, but was a neighborhood of loose kinship networks spread over the hills and bottomlands.

East Texas, therefore, was Mexican in soil but Anglo-American in culture. Among its several districts were to be found the half-Indian hunter and trader, the restless and the shiftless, the earnest colonist and the crass speculator, the whisky peddler and the itinerant preacher, and all the other classic types of the Southern frontier. Over-all a population which was rural, egalitarian, independent, individualistic, aggressive, and adaptable, it was, in some localities, through the selective processes of the political border, volatile and conspiratorial as well.

Between Bexar and Nacogdoches lay the Department of Brazoria, Mexican in frame and American in substance. That it was American in population obviously set it off sharply from bordering Bexar, that these Americans came within a more explicit influence of Mexican institutions set it off importantly if much less sharply from East Texas. A critical difference was the dominant influence of the *empresario* system. That settlers were in some degree recruited, at least nominally selected, and then carefully allocated lands was in marked contrast to the uncontrolled folk-movement infiltration characteristic of the country east of the Trinity. The assurance of title to a large tract of land, the confidence inspired by so tireless and effective an intermediary with the Mexican government as Stephen F. Austin, and the attractions of such a fine country so advantageously located, all combined to lure a good many colonists of high quality and at least some with ample means as well. That some of these persons were seeking asylum as well as land was very likely, but they at least had the conditions of their aslyum spelled out to them and every landholder had to give formal allegiance to Mexico and her laws. The result was certainly a more stable society than that of Nacogdoches and one whose members were strongly concentrated on the economic development of their own properties.

The towns, too, reflected a Mexican influence in plan but were strongly Anglo-American in character. Some, such as Gonzales, with its gridiron of inner and outer lots, its five public squares and its plaza, were quite elaborate in design, and almost all exhibited the common Hispanic elements. Yet their inhabitants had so little sense of such civic order that San Felipe, for example, though formal in plan was so American in appearance as to shock a Mexican visitor: "the houses are not arranged systematically so as to form streets; but on the contrary, lie in an irregular and desultory manner." That San Felipe, first in being, central in location, and the capital of Austin's huge realm, remained to the end of the Mexican period little more than a rude scattering of log cabins was further testimony of the rural predilections of these colonists. As a Mexican visitor of 1834 commented, the place had increased little in a decade "because the Anglo-Americans do not like to build large towns where there is land for expansion." But some towns such as Brazoria, Columbia, and Matagorda did grow, and these were equally typical of the Anglo-American frontier process. Each was a port arising to serve a hinterland (the first two serving the same, Columbia developing as sickness drove many persons from Brazoria), and thus each illustrated the fact that for such a people the town was not a primary, formal, and administrative creation but was a secondary, speculative response to commercial opportunity.

Thus Mexican Texas, in the course of its fifteen-year career, was altered from a land of two incipient regional cultures to a land of three. On balance, of course, Brazoria and Nacogdoches had much in common, and ultimately the combined weight and geographic position of these two underlay the course of the Texas Revolution. Not that the conflict itself was primarily a civil war amongst Texas peoples, between those of Bexar and those of the other two regions, for it was rather a war between the Mexican state, represented by its armies from beyond the Rio Grande, and the Anglo-American colonists. But the great imbalance in size of population and area, between the four thousand in a few clusters in the relatively narrow strip of Bexar and the more than twenty thousand spread thinly over the breadth of the other two, was certainly relevant to the outcome. It was not merely accidental that the two great Anglo-American disasters, at the Alamo and Goliad, took place beyond the margins of Anglo-American colonization, while their final triumph, at San Jacinto, took place deep within a country they had made their own.

Chapter II

★ ASSERTION

~~~~~~

ALL INTERPRETERS OF TEXAS AGREE THAT THE TEN YEARS OF
the Republic had an immense psychological impact. As a recent
analyst of the "Texas myth" has put it, the importance of the
simple fact of independence "has been indelibly stamped upon
the memory of the Texan (he can raise more hell on Texas
Independence Day than on the Fourth of July) and upon the
folk memory of the non-Texan as well." These years were basic
and formative, and out of them a recognizable "Texas culture"
first began to assume a coherent pattern. And these years of
independence were also a geographically creative period, in
which certain incipient areal patterns, certain regional differ-
entiations, certain functional orientations and spatial networks
of circulation were of a character which made the human
geography of the Texas of 1845 a recognizable forerunner of
the Texas of today.

However, while 1836 was an abrupt change of sharp significance, 1845 had relatively little direct impact upon such
matters. Just as the flag of the Republic became the flag of the
state and "its clear symbol of a single star" continued to be
"proudly flown to represent a state that is independent, solitary
and unique," so the geographical patterns and trends of the Republic were simply extended and elaborated on into statehood
with little interruption or alteration. Such developments continued until 1861, when many of them were abruptly stopped

or changed. The next several years were a period of stagnation and even retrogression. Furthermore, by the eve of that interim Texas had reached an important phase in the course of her geographical development which deserves careful depiction. Thus the quarter of a century between the revolt against Mexico and the revolt against the United States can be appropriately examined as a single era of development which culminates in an important over-all geographical pattern.

A. EMPIRE

The leaders of the new Texas Republic laid claim to an area far greater than the Texas of Spain or Mexico. By insisting upon the whole course of the Rio Grande as the southern and western boundary, they asserted dominion over half of New Mexico and extended their reach from the Gulf of Mexico to the Southern Rockies (Map 5). Although the area was very largely devoid of civilized settlement, and was quite beyond the resources of the young nation even to explore, and beyond the power of the young state to retain in its entirety, such pretentions did involve the Texans briefly but significantly with the long-rooted Hispano-Indian population of New Mexico, caused Texas leaders and promoters to see a link to Santa Fe as a logical part of her development, and gave an important impetus to the persistent Texan dream of empire.

In actual fact, the Republic was never able to establish control over even the nearest portion of its new claim. Apart from a single expedition to Laredo and the lower Rio Grande, Texas power was never applied beyond the Nueces, and that expedition was itself only a retaliation for the brief but humiliating seizure of San Antonio, Goliad, and Refugio by invading Mexican forces. Uncontrolled by either side, the Trans-Nueces country became a no man's land in which "mustangers" and "prairie pirates" stole horses and cattle, smuggled goods, and robbed and murdered travellers with impunity—a dreaded Desierto Muerto. It remained dangerous country even after recognition of the Rio Grande as the boundary was forced upon Mexico as a result of the war of 1846, although the presence of a few federal garrisons and the rise of Corpus Christi and Brownsville

as new commercial centers began to bring some security to its
margins. However, except for the latter town, the Valley remained an area almost entirely Hispano-American, isolated
and alien, annexed entirely through extrinsic interests, sheltering refugees from both contestants, and responsive in some degree to recurrent secessionist schemes in northeastern Mexico.
It was a severed half of old Nuevo Santandar, a vivid exhibit
of the truth of Texas as an empire: a people and a country conquered and ruled but restive and unassimilated.

Although Texas failed to capture the only other major civilized district within her new imperial claims, her interests in
that far western realm persisted. The idea of binding Santa Fe
to the Texas Gulf was no sudden enlargement of Texas horizons
in 1836. Evidently Moses Austin's original plan in seeking permission for a colony in Texas was primarily to establish a base
for tapping the New Mexican trade. Although his son shifted
the emphasis from commerce to agriculture, he did not lose
sight of the former. In 1824 a company of French merchants
actually carried goods from Copano Bay to Santa Fe at great
profit, but fear of the Comanches and the new competition
from Missouri kept them from continuing. But Stephen Austin
expressed the view of many when he insisted that "the geographical situation of the country and nature itself" clearly
"marked out" the ocean ports of Texas, not the river towns of
Missouri, as the logical base for the Santa Fe trade. The Republic of Texas sent three different expeditions to assert some measure of control over Santa Fe and its commerce and each was an
ignominious failure, yet in the fluid aftermath of the 1846
United States triumph over Mexico some Texan leaders envisioned an even further westward reach and all firmly insisted
upon at least their original Rio Grande claim. In 1849 the Texas
legislature divided its imperial western borderlands into counties and was well underway with local organization in New
Mexico before the final compromise was reached whereby debt-
ridden Texas withdrew to her present western boundary in
return for a ten million dollar indemnification. The particular
geographical design came out of a welter of proposals and was
more a result of compromises among various factions of the

Map 4

"New Map of Texas with the Contiguous American and Mexican States, By J. H. Young." Philadelphia: published by S. Augustus Mitchell, 1835.

(Courtesy of the Archives, State Historical Society of Wisconsin)

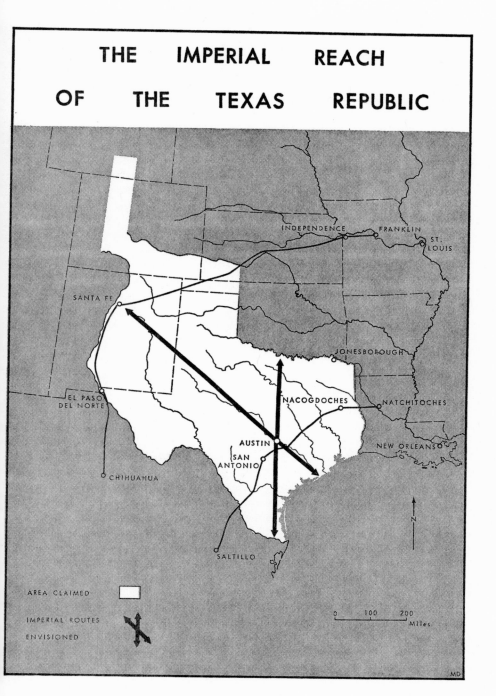

THE IMPERIAL REACH
OF THE TEXAS REPUBLIC

ST. LOUIS

INDEPENDENCE   FRANKLIN

SANTA FE

JONESBOROUGH

EL PASO
DEL NORTE

NACOGDOCHES   NATCHITOCHES

AUSTIN   NEW ORLEANS

SAN
ANTONIO

CHIHUAHUA

N

SALTILLO

AREA CLAIMED

IMPERIAL ROUTES
ENVISIONED

0   100   200
Miles

MD

Map 5

national Congress than of direct negotiations with Texas. It does reflect its times, however, for that long corridor to El Paso del Norte had suddenly been made immeasurably more important by the gold-rush traffic to California and the excitement over transcontinental railroads. Thus a strong Texas interest was maintained in this direction and the thrust as far west as Tucson and the seizure of (but soon forced withdrawal from) Albuquerque and Santa Fe in the opening years of the Civil War was more a reassertion of Texas imperialism than an integral part of Confederate strategy.

This imperial concept was indelibly expressed in the selection of the location for the capital of the new nation in 1839. In terms of the settlement and trafficways of the time Houston or some site in that vicinity certainly had the most convincing claims. But the men who were finally empowered to resolve this heated issue found their logic in the geography of the future rather than in that of the present: "The Commissioners confidently anticipate the time when a great thoroughfare shall be established from Santa Fe to our seaports, and another from Red River to Matamoros, which two routs [*sic*] must always of necessity intersect each other at this point." Sited at the contact between "the green romantic Mountains, and the fertile and widely extended plains," they considered Austin to be a beautiful setting at once strategic and symbolic (Map 5). Placing the seat of government upon the very edge of settlement would serve to impress an expansive vision upon the minds of the whole citizenry and accelerate migration to the west, thereby soon bringing better protection against the Comanche. The Republic authorized national military roads along the routes mentioned, as well as an important branch to link the capital with the Red River settlements in the far corner. But these were quite beyond her resources to build, and in 1845 Austin was still entirely marginal rather than at all pivotal in the developing geography of the nation.

B. INFLOW

Independence accelerated immigration. Although the new government reduced the size of land allotments to newcomers the amount was still so much greater and the price so much lower than in the United States as to prove very attractive. It was a migration which drew strongly from the whole breadth of the South, bringing into Texas three general streams of movement whose sources reached back two generations and more to the Atlantic seaboard. The northernmost can be traced from southeastern Pennsylvania, western Maryland, and Virginia across to Kentucky and the Ohio Valley, touching southern Indiana and Illinois, and on to Missouri and Arkansas. The middle stream flowed out of Virginia and the Carolinas into Tennessee and thence across Arkansas, while the southern linked the Carolinas to Alabama, Mississippi, and Louisiana. The last two of these three flows were the more important. As a leading Texas student of this migration summarized: "the typical East Texan derived from the back-country folk of the Carolinas, and the pivot of his westward progression had been either Tennessee or Alabama." And he was more likely to have come to Texas directly from such pivotal states than from Arkansas or Louisiana, for Texas was settled more by long-distant migrants than by progressive infiltration from just across its borders.

Although converging upon Northeast Texas, these three migrations tended to pass through separate portals (Fulton, Arkansas; Jefferson; and Nacogdoches, respectively) and flow into separate districts, forming northern, middle, and southern areas within Texas concordant with the general Southern source regions (Map 6). But these were not rigid channels; in detail there was much intermingling, and especially as the frontier of settlement was pushed westward there was a complex interlacing with some landseekers spreading from the coastal plain up the Neches and the Trinity, the Navasota and the Brazos, all the way to the Cross Timbers, while others worked their way southwestward from the Red River across these same streams into the central hills.

A fourth line of migration was that entering directly from the Gulf of Mexico. New Orleans, the commercial entrepôt for so large a part of the nation, drew migrants bound for Texas from an equally large hinterland, although, in keeping with the overland patterns, the flow was heavier from the Gulf states on

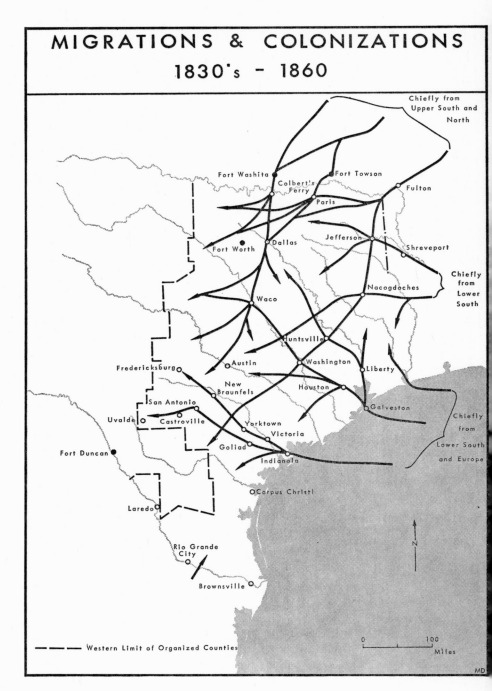

MIGRATIONS & COLONIZATIONS
1830's - 1860

Chiefly from
Upper South and
North

Fort Washita
Colbert's
Ferry
Fort Towson
Fulton
Paris

Fort Worth
Dallas
Jefferson
Shreveport

Chiefly
from
Lower
South

Nacogdoches

Waco

Huntsville

Fredericksburg
Austin
Washington
Liberty

New
Braunfels
Houston

San Antonio

Uvalde
Castroville
Yorktown
Galveston

Chiefly
from
Lower South
and Europe

Victoria
Goliad
Indianola

Fort Duncan

Corpus Christi

Laredo

Rio Grande
City

Brownsville

N

Western Limit of Organized Counties

0   100
Miles

Map 6

the east than from the river states on the north. But of greater significance was the inflow of European migrants, at times whole shiploads of them, to the Texan ports. Though fewer in numbers they were so different in culture as to leave a sharp imprint upon every area they touched.

For the most part, all these overland migrations were unorganized folk movements responding to the lure of letters and rumors, channelled complexly by the varieties of country and the networks of family and friends. At this time Texas granted land by acreage units, leaving the settler, upon certification, free to measure out his land upon any part of the unappropriated domain, uncontrolled by the basic framework of any survey system. It was the Texan version of the old Southern system. But the other source of the Texan tradition was also clearly apparent in the several modified *empresario* grants authorized by the Republic. Although there was a general Anglo antipathy to any infringement upon the right of a man to settle wherever he wished, it was overbalanced by the very great anxiety over Comanche raids. A combination of battles and negotiations cleared the Indians from all east of the Cross Timbers by the early 1840's, but this left a long western frontier still dangerously exposed. Thus a series of large grants was made to contractors who offered to settle large numbers of colonists within a short period of time along that frontier. The most important of these resulted in the Peters Colony, a wholly Anglo-American venture, along the headwaters of the Trinity; in the Castro Colony of Alsatians in a narrow fertile belt along the base of the Balcones Escarpment just west of San Antonio; and, in between these two, in a large German colony deep in the Hill Country west of Austin. Each of these was initiated in the last years of the Republic and was continued during the early years of statehood, and each soon brought greater security to its area and served as a nucleus for further expansion for years afterward.

In 1836 the pioneers had barely touched the great longitudinal belt of the black prairie lands which cuts a widening swath from Bexar to the Red River; by 1845 they were penetrating the Eastern Cross Timbers on the north and probing the Hill

Country on the south, and thus in the concepts of the time, had
encompassed the whole (north of the Nueces) of the "level"
and "undulating" regions and reached the edge of the "moun-
tainous" lands. The first line of federal forts erected to protect
the frontier, reaching from Fort Worth to Fort Duncan at
Eagle Pass, clearly marked that advance. By 1860 the vanguard
was a hundred miles or more farther west, where the rougher
timbered land gave way to broadening brushy plains (Map 7).
Although half of Texas still lay beyond, and the Comanches
still roamed at will over "the vast ocean of prairie" above the
Caprock, the general limits of settlement had been doubled in
twenty-five years, and a line of federal forts now reached from
the Red River to El Paso, shielding the trails to California.

C. Provinces

The patterns of cultural geography had also been significantly modified by the various events and migrations of those years.
The revolt against Mexico itself had an immediate impact, for
much of the Hispano population was driven out of Bexar, and
took refuge along the Rio Grande or beyond. The loss of all the
officials and most persons of property meant an even more
drastic change in character than in numbers. With this defor-
mation of Bexar, the well-rooted regional consciousness of
Nacogdoches and Brazoria was enlarged to divide the whole of
Texas between the two and to dominate the national politics of
the Republic. This produced a cleavage that was accentuated
by the role of Sam Houston, the most famous and controversial
figure of the new nation and the acknowledged folk hero of
East Texas; legislators came to be referred to as "Eastern" or
"Western" according to their bias for or against Houston's policies. Geographically this regionalism was best expressed in the
contest over the location of the national capital. East Texas
threw its weight behind the town of Houston. Located on the
tidewater between the Trinity and Brazos, it was a new town,
coeval with the Republic, bound by tradition neither to East
nor West and well placed to serve them both. Even after Austin
had been finally selected and the government actually estab-

lished there, Sam Houston, during his second term, tried to shift it back to this rising commercial center on the Gulf.

This cleavage persisted; Olmsted reported from his travels of 1856 that "the vaguest tavern conversation assumes a natural antagonism and future division between Eastern and Western Texas." But as he well knew and described in his book Texas was more culturally varied than this simple dualism suggested. By 1860 four broad regions and numerous enclaves could be discerned (Map 8).

With statehood East Texas was no longer a sanctuary for those fleeing the laws elsewhere and the developments of each year brought a greater homogeneity and stability. Although there was a continual influx of people it brought little variety, for, except for a small infiltration of Creoles west of the lower Sabine, it was entirely Anglo-American and very largely from Alabama and other Gulf states. East Texas was thus the western extension of the older Deep South and it had evolved fully in accordance with the patterns of its source region. Whereas it early displayed all the elements common to the backwoods frontier, it now displayed all those common to the patchwork of prosperity and poverty characteristic of the older states. It had an economy based upon cotton, corn, cattle, and hogs, a wholly rural society focused upon agrarian ideals, in which slaves, who made up a third or more of the total population, were an integral part of the economic and social structure (Map 8). There were great differences from place to place in the proportions of such elements. Where soils and transport were favorable, cotton dominated the land, slaves were numerous, towns had developed at shipping points, and the society as a whole lived in regular contact with New Orleans and the wider world, while back in the piney woods and swamplands the squatter and hunter were still scattered in isolated pockets with only the most tenuous connections to commercial society. Most of the population lived a life in between these extremes: small farmers, small slaveowners, raising a little cotton and a few head of livestock, living in some contact with one another and within reach of at least a county-seat hamlet. Despite the

wide gradations in wealth and refinement it was a single culture, sprung from the same roots and shaped by the same forces,
in which rich and poor, slaveowner and squatter, were members of the same widely extended families. The one class was
as directly linked to the other as the crude "dog-trot" log cabin
was related to the handsome center-hallway plantation home:
extremes of the same genre.

To the northwest of this old East Texas region another had
emerged which was not sharply set off, yet which was recognized at the time as distinct. It lay beyond the headwaters of
the Sabine and extended rather narrowly southward along the
rich Blackland Prairies. It was distinctly Border South country,
drawing most heavily from Missouri, strongly from Arkansas
and Tennessee, and significantly from Illinois. In the very
midst of the region were the lands of the Peters Colony, with
settlers recruited almost entirely from these same states. For
several years such lands could be sold only to non-Texans, and
thus the colony developed as an enclave with some common
background but no direct population ties with East Texas. Furthermore, it had an interesting enclave within itself in the several hundred French who in 1855 attempted to establish the
Fourier socialist colony of La Reunion on the upper Trinity
just west of the young town of Dallas. The experiment soon
failed and some of the members moved to the town.

In 1860 Dallas was no larger than several other towns in the
region, but it was already noticeably superior in certain quali-
ties. For typical of such idealistic schemes, La Reunion had
brought to the frontier people with an uncommon degree of
education, refinement, and initiative. Although the colony
failed partly because it had too many teachers, musicians,
chemists, and surgeons and too few farmers and laborers, such
people gave a strong impetus to civic life in Dallas, and their
fellow craftsmen are credited with being the first to establish
in the town such useful things as a tailor shop, brewery, brick-
yard, lime kiln, and carriage and wagon works. Such cultural
variety and such an array of skills were to be found nowhere
else in this otherwise rather homogeneous region and were
surely an important, if unmeasurable, influence in the subse-

Map 7

"Johnson's New Map of the State of Texas,
by Johnson and Ward [1863]."
(Courtesy of the Archives, University of Texas)

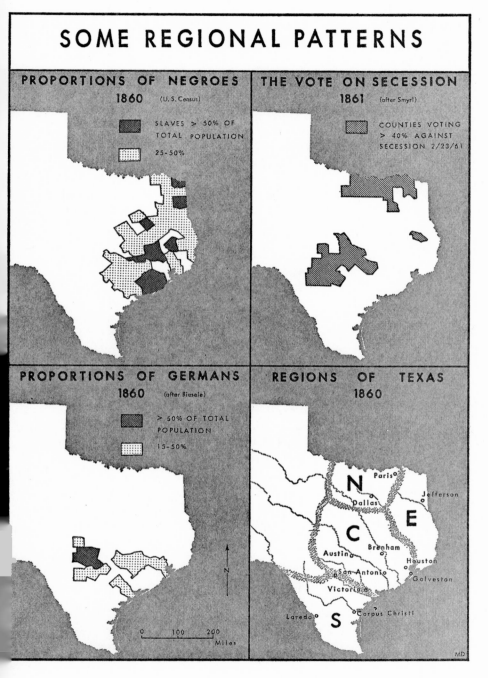

SOME REGIONAL PATTERNS

PROPORTIONS OF NEGROES
1860 (U. S. Census)

SLAVES > 50% OF TOTAL POPULATION

25-50%

THE VOTE ON SECESSION
1861 (after Smyrl)

COUNTIES VOTING > 40% AGAINST SECESSION 2/23/61

PROPORTIONS OF GERMANS
1860 (after Biesele)

> 50% OF TOTAL POPULATION

15-50%

0   100   200
Miles

REGIONS OF TEXAS
1860

N

Paris

Dallas

Jefferson

E

C

Austin

Brenham

San Antonio

Houston

Victoria

Galveston

Laredo

Corpus Christi

S

N

Map 8

quent emergence of the city. But Dallas, initiated by a lawyer-merchant from Tennessee, also exhibited the Border South in its very form: platted separately by two adjacent landowners, each section in a simple grid, but thirty degrees askew to one another and unintegrated—a basically Middle Western plan deformed by the random survey system of the South and the frontier insistence upon individual property rights without regard to the whole.

North Texas in general differed rather markedly from East Texas in the relative unimportance of cotton and the relatively few slaves. The extent to which this was an expression of economic possibilities rather than cultural preferences is not determinable, but it was a difference which would have important political implications. In general, also, agriculture was more diversified, with a greater emphasis upon wheat and oats than corn; settlement was more compact; towns a more vital part of social organization; and the contrasts between rich and poor rather less prominent. In short, there existed here between North and East Texas the same difference as that between Kentucky and Alabama.

To the west and south of these two regions was another which may conveniently be called Central Texas, although in 1860 that term was used, if at all, for a smaller area within. It was essentially old Brazoria with an extension into the western hills, and its main nucleus was still anchored in the rich bottomlands of the early Austin Colony. The Trinity River was still commonly regarded as the border between Central and East Texas, but it was in some ways less of a cultural divide than before. The institutional differences of the Mexican era had faded in significance and the human differences among the Southern immigrants on either side were perhaps even more subtle. The most obvious contrast was the fact that, whereas the neighboring part of East Texas was the poorest piney-woods country, the rich and accessible coastal plain and the best of the bottomlands upriver continued to attract men of capital. Alabamans and others came in with money to buy land and with tools and slaves ready to work it. Added to Austin's pioneer families who had successfully transformed their leagues of wilderness into productive estates, later arrivals made the sugar and cotton lands of the coastal counties and the Brazos Valley the seat of a class of citizens who were wealthy and influential beyond any group to the east. In such districts Negroes made up more than half, in places as much as 80 percent, of the population, and Southern whites of all levels were touched by the economic success and the social prestige of the slave plantation.

But in 1860 the Brazos was a more obvious cultural boundary than the Trinity. To the east, whatever the local differences, all was Anglo-American and African, entirely Southern in origin; to the west, in almost every district, European settlers were vividly evident and added a new complexity to the social geography. The principal root of this development reached back into Mexican Texas to a single German settler, who came to the Austin Colony in 1831 and soon began to sing the praises of Texas in letters home. By 1836 his efforts had recruited a small group of Germans to the low rolling woodlands and prairies west of San Felipe, between the Brazos and the Colorado. Germans continued to be drawn to the area and they had soon spread over several counties, forming loose neighborhoods between and amongst those of the Anglo-Americans. Thus Oldenburg, Weimar, and New Ulm appeared on the maps amidst such characteristically American names as Cat Spring, Round Top, and Columbus, and German settlers could be found in all. By 1860 they constituted nearly a quarter of the population over a broad district (Map 8).

Considerably larger numbers of Europeans came in as a result of the Republic's group colonization program. Henri Castro recruited more than two thousand settlers from the Franco-German borderlands and firmly implanted his Alsatian village in the valley of the Medina. Many drifted off to San Antonio and elsewhere, but enough took root there and in neighboring valleys to give an indelible character to a whole district. A much larger program was undertaken by the German company which was granted a large tract deep in the Hill Country. In order to move colonists into the area the company first established a port, Indianola (Carlshafen, to them), and a way station, New Braunfels. The latter, laid out on a small prairie in rich rolling country at the base of the hills, was so much more attractive than the main area granted, that it became the major nucleus. By the end of its first year, 1845, New Braunfels was a thriving community of fifteen hundred people, with an array of stores and shops, professions and craftsmen, a church and a school. It became the main center from which several thousand more Germans spread into other districts, and it was from the first an exhibit of a type of community and a colonization process strikingly different from anything carried out by the Anglo-Americans in the vicinity. Within two years the company had put two thousand settlers in and around the new town of Fredericksburg in the upper Pedernales country, and they soon spread clear to the Llano, a hundred miles beyond New Braunfels and well beyond the Anglo frontier of the time. Meanwhile, other Germans, some in organized groups as at Yorktown, more as individuals and families, as around Victoria and Seguin, had settled in various localities along the route between the Gulf and the hills. By 1860 such colonists placed a strong German stamp upon the life and landscape of a broad strip of country reaching from Indianola to the San Saba.

In the 1850's this European imprint was somewhat enlarged and significantly varied by the arrival of Slavic families who followed in the wake of and settled amongst the Germans, chiefly in the Brazos and Colorado districts and along the San Antonio River outside the lands of the colonization companies. There were Bohemians and Moravians (Czechs) and Sorbians (Wends), largely Lutheran, and Silesian Poles, Roman Catholics—all of whom came from German-ruled homelands but who maintained in Texas as in Europe their separate identities.

And there was a sprinkling of further variety: a splinter sect of American Mormons, struggling to survive in the Hill Country above Austin; for a brief time an experimental English colony at the City of Kent in Bosque County in the vague borderlands of Central and North Texas, and, more solidly and just below the English, a group of Norwegian Lutherans. None of these had a lasting effect upon any considerable district, but, together with the thousands of Germans, Alsatians, Czechs, and Poles, they displayed at the time the general cultural variety so characteristic of Central Texas and so little evident to the north and east.

It was a variety vivid in the life and landscape of the region. Some reference to the most general contrast, between the Southern American and the German, was part of most every traveller's report. Both worked with cotton, corn, and livestock, but the sprawling slave-worked plantation, devoted to cotton, with meager attention to anything else and more acreage in waste than in crop, was as certain an indication of the one as the much smaller, family operated, diversified farm of field and pasture, garden, orchard, and vineyard, was of the other. Such farms would be gross exaggerations of more common differences, but some such contrast was almost always readily discernible. Slaves were not a sure mark of the American, but relatively few Germans used them, there was widespread antipathy and some strong opposition to doing so, and slaves were certainly not, as with their Southern neighbors, viewed as a mark of prestige and a most appropriate means to success. The Southern crossroads hamlet or county seat and the German market-centered town were equally obvious exhibits: the one a loose sprawl of log or clapboard cabins, with perhaps a modest Greek Revival house or two graced with a bit of New Orleans ironwork; the other a neat arrangement of wide streets compactly lined with stone or stuccoed cottages, with perhaps a bit of *fachwerk* (half-timbering) showing or some startling bit of European design, as in the octagonal church of Fredericksburg, or the hexagonal home of that very first German settler in the Austin Colony, who built a replica of his Oldenburg summer house (he had been the chief gardener of an estate). Olmsted was a biased observer, obviously happy with the good food and solid comfort he found among the Germans after a long succession of rather squalid Southern country houses and inns, but his contrast between a Gonzales, which still lay gaunt in its Mexican frame with "the usual square of dead bare land, surrounded by a collection of stores, shops, drinking and gambling rooms, a court-house, and a public-house or two, with the nearly vacant mapped streets behind," and a New Braunfels, less than half as old, but with broad streets thickly lined with comfortable houses and a veritable beehive of small industries, was an appropriate emphasis. It was of course a contrast between a strongly rural, militantly independent, mobile, and aggressive people nurtured on the frontier, and a strongly community-minded people drawn from the rigidly ordered countrysides and villages of Europe who came in groups and clung together as an alien minority. While the one seemed to be largely a fluid, unstable assemblage of opportunists, the other, from its very initiation in Texas, was a remarkable interlocking network of organized clubs and societies. Again, the contrast can be exaggerated. Some Germans, happy to shed the confinements of the homeland, sought quick assimilation and there was some rapid cultural borrowing of the one from the other, in dress and diet, crops and houses. The Europeans, for example, soon learned from their American neighbors who had lived much longer in the subtropics the value of wide verandas and porches; and probably most of their villages were loose assemblages more like those of their Southern neighbors than those of their old-country kin. But even where they shared the same towns and lived in houses of similar style they remained apart in language, religion, and intimate society; Lutheran and Catholic churches and schools served the one, Methodist, Baptist, Presbyterian, and Campbellite the other. In general, neither group had much admiration for the other; the Germans considered the Americans to be shiftless, greedy, and undependable, and were, in return, considered clannish, loutish, and dull. It was not a bitter antagonism, but it was a firm social cleavage.

On the southern edge of Central Texas remnants of the Mexican past created still another facet of variety. By 1860 the Anglos had gotten control, by fair means or foul, of nearly every ranch worth having north of the Nueces, but they still needed a few vaqueros to work them. Travellers often commented on the "Mexican ranches" of the area, so different in appearance from an Anglo or European settlement, but it is clear that the term still referred to the *rancheria*, the crude hut and brush-fenced yard of the Mestizo family with its sheep and goats. Clusters of these were scattered over the area but most of the Hispano-American population was to be found along the Indianola-San Antonio road, a trafficway on which large numbers were employed as carters, packers, and drovers. Skirting the northern edge of the mesquite plains, that highway bisected a complex cultural border zone. Cattle and cotton were the mainstays of much of Central Texas, but it was only here that the plantation and the hacienda, the two great patriarchal landed institutions richly idealized by the contending cultures, really met. But it was an unbalanced encounter of forces, and the military triumph of the one drove out the leadership of the other, so that both institutions were now ruled by the Anglo, the one worked by the Negro slave, the other still worked by the Mestizo vaquero.

The social geography of the area was complex and unstable. East of Victoria nearly all of the few Hispanos who had not fled in 1836 were harassed and driven out in 1845 or shortly thereafter. To the west Anglo and Hispano lived physically adjacent, but socially separate, in some places within the frame of a single town, in others each in his own, as at Goliad and La Bahia, the new Anglo town and the Mexican village around the old Spanish ruins, or, similarly, at Helena and Alamita. Victoria, the largest town and the main focus of the cattle and cotton economies of this coastal district, was also a good exhibit of its cultural variety, with Anglos, Germans, Negroes, and Hispanos in about equal proportions. By 1860 six denominations—Roman Catholic, Methodist, Presbyterian, Lutheran, Baptist, and Episcopalian (in order of establishment)—were holding services, a religious variety characteristic of South Central Texas and markedly different from other regions. Further south the Irish Catholics of Refugio and San Patricio had spread well beyond their initial locales. By 1860 a widely spaced arc of towns from the Gulf to the Balcones Escarpment—Corpus Christi-San Patricio-Beeville-Pleasanton-Uvalde —marked the advance of settlement and security onto the plains of South Texas. Even so, a hundred miles or more of dangerous wilderness still separated the Nueces country from the lower Rio Grande, and it had rather effectively insulated most of the settlements along the river from much encroachment. Aside from a small garrison, Laredo remained entirely an Hispano-American town. But downriver, once a military foothold was obtained, the distance and dangers of the land were easily circumvented by sea; and, thus, near the Gulf entryway Brownsville had grown up rapidly in the shelter of Fort Brown (established in 1846). In 1860 its population was largely Hispano, but it was nevertheless dominated by Anglo merchants, shippers, and politicians. As in the Nueces country, the Anglos pressed hard to obtain control of the choicest ranches, but here they were up against a much more compact body of Hispanos much less disorganized by the warfare of 1836 and 1845. Thus the Anglos were less successful, and so crass and corrupt were their attempts that they ignited a violent revolt among the Hispanos in 1859, the suppression of which could only further embitter the relations between the two peoples.

These regions within Texas—East, North, Central, and South —are to be thought of as gross generalizations rather than distinct entities, but are nonetheless essential to any characterization of Texas culture. They were certainly relevant in some degree to the whole gamut of social and political issues—local, state, and national. This was apparent, for example, in the national crisis of 1861. The fact that the governor's message and reports of the convention over secession were officially issued in English, German, and Spanish editions was a clear indication of the importance of three cultures, while the vote held exclusively on that issue, on February 23, 1861, clearly revealed the general existence if not any exact boundaries of three of the four culture regions described (Map 8). The fourth, South Texas, was obscured simply because few Hispano-Americans bothered or were able to vote and the issue had little meaning to those who feared any kind of Anglo government.

D. Cities

The chief cities of Texas lay within the blurred border zones of some of these regions and they not only displayed something of the elements of the cultures nearby but helped to draw these together and mediate their differences. Houston and Galveston, fifty miles apart and in some degree rivals, were to a larger degree a functional pair, the one the tidewater focus and the other the ocean port, linked across the waters of Galveston Bay, binding much of East and Central Texas to the commerce and culture of America and Europe. They were complementary in many ways: the one in intimate contact with a wide rural hinterland, the other looking across the seas to New Orleans, New York, and London; the one devoted very largely to business, the other very considerably to culture and leisure. The populations of both displayed all the variety of their hinterlands and more, with New Englanders and New Yorkers, English and Scotch, French and Italians added to the Anglos and Negroes, Germans, Czechs, and Irish of the countryside. Here Episcopalians and Lutherans, Catholics and Jews together overshadowed the Methodists and Baptists, who were so dominant over so large a part of the interior. While Houston, on the muddy banks of Buffalo Bayou, was an effective focal point for much of East and Central Texas, Galveston, strung along the strand at the tip of its narrow island, was very much detached from the rural back country. It was the main seat of shippers and bankers and of consuls from a dozen foreign nations, and it had a visual and social character quite its own. In its handsome cast-iron business fronts; its glistening rows of white houses set upon their stilts, with porches, galleries, and ornaments; its tropical trees and shrubs and flowers; its German breads, citrus fruits, and local seafoods; its variety of churches, schools, and societies; in the whole structure and fashion of its community life, Galveston was not so much a culmination of Texan culture as a combination of Texas wealth and the elements of many cultures, a product impressive and unusual to Texans and foreigners alike.

San Antonio, the only other city of comparable size, was equally distinct, but more obviously a product of its local regions, and clearly exhibited a long past as well as rapid recent growth. It was the meeting point of two regions and four peoples. All four—Hispano, Anglo, Negro, and German—were colorfully intermingled on the main streets and plazas, but they were rather sharply different in residence and occupation, diet and dress, language and religion; and Olmsted, like other visitors of the time, found this "contrast of nationalities" and "singular composite character of the town" to be "palpable" and fascinating. Approached from the northeast, the very first glimpse was striking: over the brow of a low hill "the domes and white clustered dwellings" of the compact city suddenly appeared, "basking in the edge of a vast plain." Between that view and the city itself the traveller entered the chapparal, the broad mesquite plains of South Texas. Yet that particular road (from New Braunfels) led directly into a street more typical of Central Texas: a long row of German houses, "of fresh square-cut blocks of creamy limestone, mostly of a single story and humble proportions, but neat, and thoroughly roofed and finished." At the first plaza the scene changed abruptly to "all Mexican": the battered Baroque facade of the Alamo, the windowless jacales "of stakes, plastered with mud and roofed with river-grass, or tule; or low, windowless, but better thatched, houses of adobe (gray, unburnt bricks), with groups of brown idlers lounging at their doors." Across the river on Commerce Street American houses, standing back from the street, "with galleries and jalousies and a garden picket-fence against the walk" dominated the scene, which quickly dissolved into a composite of all three cultures around the main plaza: American hotels and glass-fronted stores; German shops with German signs; low, flat-roofed Hispano stone and adobe buildings washed in blue and yellow. The Hispano-Americans, chiefly congregating in the south and southwest sectors of the city along the river and the Laredo road, were very largely employed in the freighting business; the Germans were mostly mechanics, craftsmen, shopkeepers, and a few local farmers; the Americans ran the government and most of the hotels and taverns, and controlled most of the money. The city had lost much of its population after the Revolution, but had grown rapidly after the War with Mexico, in large part because of government expenditures. It was a major military base, the outfitting place for a long string of forts in the interior, the departure point for caravans to Chihuahua and California, as well as the trade center of its local region.

North Texas, devoid of any Hispanic civic heritage, having no governmental center and as yet no basis for a commercial focus, had no city. Of the dozen or so towns, Paris was the largest and Dallas the most unusual but there was in 1860 little to indicate which, if any, of these would emerge as a regional center. This open competitive situation among a considerable number of relatively evenly spaced, similarly situated towns was very much in keeping with the rather Midwestern frontier character of the region as a whole.

E. Circulation

The developing commercial geography of these years was somewhat discordant with these political and cultural patterns. Whereas Austin was founded as central within an envisioned empire, Houston and Galveston arose at points strategic to the patterns of commerce; and whereas the inflows of various peoples were so patterned as to accentuate regional differences, the flow of traffic was increasingly focused within a single expanding circulatory system. The nucleus of that system was discernible in the Republic, but strongly extended and elaborated in early statehood. The commerce of the Republic very largely followed the flows of nature downriver to the Gulf. But none of the rivers was reliably navigable for more than a few miles, and some of the ocean entrances into the numerous sheltering coastal bays were shallow, shifting, and dangerous. The fact that the best of these entrances and the largest of these bays lay just east of the richest agricultural area had led to the initiation of nearly a dozen tiny ports on or tributary to Galveston Bay by 1840. Galveston had little competition as the ocean port, but Houston emerged as the chief inland port only after a strong rivalry (especially from Harrisburg, just down the bayou). By 1860, however, its triumph had been firmly stabilized by Houston's control of the emergent railroad network. By that date, only five years after the first line had been opened, Houston was the focus of five lines from as many directions, giving her access to the Brazos (at four different points), the Colorado, the Trinity, and Galveston City. At the inland terminals of these railroads, stage

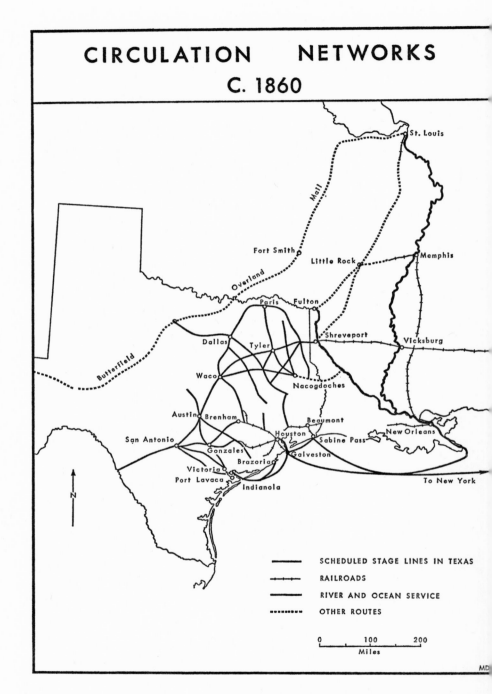

CIRCULATION NETWORKS
C. 1860

St. Louis

Mail

Fort Smith

Little Rock

Memphis

Overland

Paris

Fulton

Shreveport

Vicksburg

Dallas

Tyler

Butterfield

Waco

Nacogdoches

Austin

Brenham

Beaumont

San Antonio

Houston

Sabine Pass

New Orleans

Gonzales

Galveston

Brazoria

Victoria

Port Lavaca

Indianola

To New York

N

——————— SCHEDULED STAGE LINES IN TEXAS

+–+–+–+ RAILROADS

——————— RIVER AND OCEAN SERVICE

·········· OTHER ROUTES

0   100   200
Miles

MD

Map 9

and mail coaches linked Houston to nearly all the rest of the state. Only in the south and in the far northeast did the traffic flow in other directions (Map 9).

Houston's railroads had captured nearly all the trade of once-busy Matagorda; and Indianola and Port Lavaca were anxiously but not very effectively pushing their own railroad toward San Antonio to avoid an even more drastic diversion. Most of the commerce for San Antonio and beyond did move through these two ports and a weekly steamer gave direct service to New Orleans. However, they were linked to Galveston by a more frequent coastal service and were partially dependent upon its commercial houses. In the northeast the cotton was shipped down the Red River, the cattle were driven overland to the Mississippi, and the stage lines gave passenger and mail service to Vicksburg, Memphis, and St. Louis, linking the people of the region to their kinfolk back home and to the main interior lines of the nation. This narrow funnel of routes out of the northeast was the only important divergence from the strong Gulf orientation and Galveston Bay focus. Although a railroad link between Houston and New Orleans was being pushed, and had actually been begun at both ends, it was far from complete and paralleled no existing trafficway of importance. The whole Sabine border was a wilderness; Olmsted had found it impossible to obtain any information at all in Houston about the road east, and as he finally did make his way along an almost impassable trail he was told that "a traveler, other than a beef speculator, was a thing unknown." In the north and west the Butterfield Overland Mail, linking California to the nation, cut across seven hundred miles of Texas territory, but it was here very largely a traverse well beyond the limits of settlement and of no commercial importance to the state.

In general, therefore, in 1860 Texas displayed a fairly well integrated and very largely isolated circulatory system, connected to the outer world chiefly through Galveston, secondarily through the land and river portals in the northeast corner. It was a system expressive of the insular and provincial character of Texas as a whole. Within that whole, Spanish and Mexican patterns were still discernible, but now only as fragments enmeshed in the much more elaborate patterns which had evolved over the twenty-five years since independence. And out of those years Texans had strongly asserted and the nation had in some degree readily accepted the idea of Texas as a highly individual place and Texans as a distinctive people. The seeds of its caricature were already in vigorous growth. Triumph in war over a much larger nation, a decade of independence recognized by the leading powers of the world, statehood on its own terms, and all these within a setting huge and promising sustained a strong sense of power and individuality.

Chapter III

★ EXPANSION

~~~~~~

IN THE GENERATION FOLLOWING THE CIVIL WAR TEXAS continued to display its individuality. Although sharing much of the suffering of the whole Confederacy, Texas was physically undamaged and had attractive lands still awaiting settlement. Thus Texas was now more than ever the great Southern frontier, and despite widespread personal poverty, the postwar period was one of immigration, growth, and geographical expansion. Such a combination of internal development and frontier movement was no longer possible in the Older South; and, although here carried forth largely by sons of that Older South, it was in pattern and character more Western than Southern. And it was so largely because of the nature of the lands available for colonization: drier open country lying beyond the margins of the Southern forests. That Texans could expand so readily into such country was an expression of a heritage that was Spanish as well as Southern and a local culture that had been formed upon the borderlands of forest and prairie, of humid and dry.

So vigorous was this areal expansion that it became in fact if not in conscious design a reassertion of the old imperialism, an outreach extending the touch of Texas to lands once claimed but long since acknowledged as beyond her legal borders. Yet all the while that Texan migrants were carrying a Texan way of life into neighboring territories and Texan interests were seeking to knit those areas into the network of Texan commerce, the whole of Texas itself was being invaded by powerful interests seeking to reorient and bind Texas more directly into an aggressively expanding national network. By 1900 the issue was fully joined. Railroads from Texas had reached out and brought parts of Oklahoma, Colorado, and New Mexico, into focus upon Galveston Bay, but concomitantly railroads from the north and northeast had penetrated much of Texas, reaching south and west, cutting directly across the whole grain of the Gulf-oriented local network to bring the very borders on the Rio Grande into direct connection with St. Louis and Chicago. The innocuous general railroad map of the day, showing only a single tangled web with feeders radiating in all directions, masked the intense struggle within between a provincial and a national system. The integrity of Texas as an empire and a culture was at stake.

A. Growth

In the forty years from 1860 to 1900 the population of Texas increased fivefold. Surpassing a million in the early 1870's, it had passed three million by 1900. Much of that growth was by immigration, the tide of which ran especially heavy in the 1870's and early 1880's. As a result, in any one of those years well over half of the adult population of Texas had been born outside the state. Despite this continued heavy influx the basic character of the older regions of Texas was little altered, for the older patterns of sources, movements, and settlements persisted.

The cleavage between East Texas and North Texas in the source of settlers was perhaps even greater than before. Almost none except migrants from the Gulf states settled in the forest-lands of the East, while very few from such states moved into the Blackland Prairies and Cross Timbers of North Texas, an area which continued to receive a heavy influx from Arkansas, Missouri, and Tennessee. However, the difference in culture was probably somewhat less than such a difference in origins implied, for some of these migrants from the Border South were those most closely sympathetic to the culture of the Lower South. During the war, Marshall, Texas, became the Confederate capital-in-exile of Missouri and North Texas became an important

Maps 10a & b

The Cross Timbers and the Nueces Valley: portions of "A. R. Roessler's Latest Map of the State of Texas . . . compiled and drawn by M. Y. Mittendorfer, C.E., 1874."

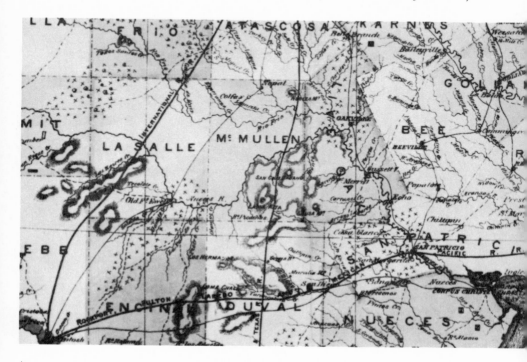

refuge area for Missouri slaveowners. It was a migration following the path of some of the earliest Anglo movements into the Southwest. Furthermore, the abolition of slavery somewhat diminished the differences among these various Southern groups, who generally agreed upon what they considered to be the proper social and economic position of the Negro and no longer need disagree about the means to effect it. Thus with the extension of railroads into the area, the raising of cotton and the use of Negro labor was soon spread well across those very counties which had so clearly opposed secession.

Central Texas continued to be an area of vigorous growth and cultural mixture. All the several streams of migration from the South sent branches into the region, and the influx from Germany, Bohemia, and Moravia was resumed after the war. These Europeans moved very largely into those localities already dominated by fellow nationals, clustering into neighborhoods and spreading out only gradually and cohesively into the Anglo areas. In 1900 they still clung rather strongly to native dress, customs, and language. German newspapers were published in more than a dozen different towns of the region, and Germans were still a major part of the population of Galveston, Houston, and San Antonio. And the unique ethnic and religious variety of the southern margins of Central Texas continued to be well displayed in Victoria. A local author of the 1880's estimated that the town was composed of Anglos, Germans, Negroes, Poles, French, and Mexicans (ranked by numbers); and in church populations of Roman Catholic, Lutheran, Presbyterian, Episcopalian, Jewish, Baptist, Methodist, and Christian.

There was immigration from south of the Rio Grande also, which gradually over these years reinforced the Hispanic character of all South Texas. The movement was sporadic, but it was never wholly checked by the recurrent brigandry in the Nueces country and persistent social antagonism between Anglo and Hispano. With the building of railroads and the fencing of the open ranges the whole region was gradually domesticated into a uniform pattern in town, farm, and ranch of Anglo rule over an Hispano population.

B. Frontier

While these regions were developing along patterns well rooted in the past, a new region was being formed in the west. This West Texas of the time was half of the entire state and it was physically varied and with settlement would become differentiated into parts. But for a time it was essentially a single region, the whole of it relatively dry and open country with common problems, dangers, and opportunities; and the initial stages of its domestication were similar from one end to the other. The removal of the Indians and the buffalo was a necessary prelude to Texan expansion, a bloody business largely completed by 1875. Federal troops operating from forts on every side, supplemented at times by Texas Rangers, gradually closed in on the High Plains and its marginal canyons, the last refuge of the Comanches; similarly and simultaneously the buffalo hunters, working out of crude temporary "hide towns," relentlessly closed in upon the last of the great Southern Plains herds. Immediately in their wake, and at times even in amongst them, came the cattlemen.

The historical geography of the range cattle industry in Texas is considerably more complex than that of the common generalization, which depicts the Nueces country as the great nursery, sending millions northward along the trails to Eastern markets and to other Western ranges. The Nueces country was certainly an important part of the pattern and it, or, more exactly, the mesquite borderlands along the San Antonio and Guadalupe rivers, was the first point of that sustained contact between Anglo and Hispano which produced the acculturation, the transfer of tools and techniques, which was obviously fundamental to the development of the industry. But the Anglos were not unfamiliar with cattle raising. Cattle herding and cattle droving were a standard part of the Southern frontier tradition reaching back to the Carolinas. The Anglo pioneers of Texas brought cattle with them and many of these settlers and their descendants, with no direct contact whatever with Hispanic culture, became or remained stockmen and not farmers. The cattle industry of the Plains was therefore a blend of two traditions.

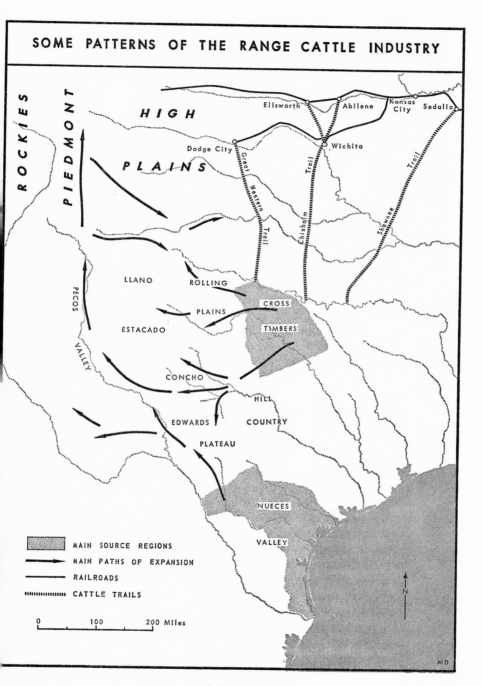

SOME PATTERNS OF THE RANGE CATTLE INDUSTRY

ROCKIES

PIEDMONT

HIGH

PLAINS

Ellsworth   Abilene   Kansas City   Sedalia

Dodge City   Wichita

Great Western Trail

Chisholm Trail

Shawnee Trail

LLANO   ROLLING

PECOS   PLAINS   CROSS

VALLEY   ESTACADO   TIMBERS

CONCHO   HILL

EDWARDS   COUNTRY

PLATEAU

NUECES

MAIN SOURCE REGIONS

MAIN PATHS OF EXPANSION

RAILROADS

CATTLE TRAILS

VALLEY

0   100   200 Miles

N

MD

Map 11

Because the Hispanos had long ago perfected the managing of large herds of half-wild cattle on semi-arid open ranges, their contribution was the more important and obvious, but the fact that the Anglos had for generations been working with smaller herds of half-wild cattle in the woods, canebrakes, and smaller prairies was also important and critical to the rapid acceptance and adaptation of Hispano methods to Anglo needs. And so, too, the herds of the two were soon mixed and blended, the Hispano contributing a hardier breed, the Anglo a meatier one, the combination resulting in an animal that could withstand the rigors of the Plains and trails and still be marketable. When it is realized that these blendings of livestock and traditions had been going on for forty years before the expansion into West Texas, the pace and the pattern of that spread becomes readily understandable, even though it does not fit the standard generalization. For it was not so much an expansion northward out of South Texas as an expansion westward out of North Texas; not primarily an advance up the Nueces onto the Edwards Plateau but an advance up the Brazos and Colorado across the Rolling Plains to the base of the Caprock. South Texas was certainly an important locale of the cattle industry, and famous names such as King and Kenedy belong to the Nueces Valley, but Goodnight, Loving, and Chisum, famous pioneers in the geographical expansion of the industry after the Civil War, came out of the Cross Timbers (Map 10).

This advance in the north was along a broad front from the Red River to the Concho, with various salients and centers important at various times (Map 11). One main thrust was out of the Cross Timbers from Jacksboro and Palo Pinto, and on beyond Fort Belknap and Fort Griffin up the divergent headwaters of the Brazos. To the south a very important nucleus was formed along the Concho where its several branches gave access to a wide radius of grassy plains. The westward reach of the Concho also allowed herds to be driven across the dry divide to the Pecos and up that valley to military and mining markets in New Mexico and Colorado; and this route was soon followed by ranchers as well as drovers. The career of Charles Goodnight, one of the men who pioneered that movement, epitomizes important geographical patterns in the development of the Texas cattle industry. Illinois-born but Texas-raised, Goodnight got started as a cattleman in the Palo Pinto country before the Civil War. In 1866 he trailed a herd from the Cross Timbers to Fort Sumner, New Mexico, by way of the Concho and Pecos, and then established a ranch in the Pecos Valley at Bosque Grande, forty miles south of that fort. A few years later he shifted north to the Colorado Piedmont near the site of Pueblo, and then in 1876, just as the last Comanches were being driven out of the Texas Panhandle, he relocated again, driving his stock from Colorado southeastward across the High Plains to a new ranch site in the shelter of Palo Duro Canyon. Goodnight was the first to establish permanent operations in the Panhandle, but he was soon joined by others, some spreading down the Canadian River from New Mexico, others moving westward from North Texas up the many branches of the Red into the broken margins of the tableland. Thus the cattlemen, like the soldiers and the hide men, conquered these High Plains of Texas by encroachment from several sides rather than by a thrust along a single front.

South Texas did contribute to the expansion of the cattle industry, but much more directly to the spread westward into the Trans-Pecos than northward into the Plains. That westward advance was somewhat delayed by the depredations of the Apaches, who were not finally quelled by Mexican and American efforts until 1880. This over-all expansion of the Texas cattle industry from different thresholds of the Western Plains caused little difference in the mode of operations but carried with it an important difference in people. For wherever Anglo stockmen spread out from South Texas, the Hispano vaquero went along to do much of the work, whereas everywhere to the north the cowboys were Anglo or Negro.

A more important regional difference in the livestock industry, rooted in these same years and enduring still, was the heavy emphasis on sheep and goats in addition to cattle on the Edwards Plateau, precisely between the two patterns of expansion of the cattle industry. This, too, developed from the contact of two cultures; it was largely a German perfection of an old Hispanic activity, growing directly out of the struggle of the

earliest German settlers to make a living out of the brushy Texas
Hill Country, teaming the industrious German stockman with
the dependable Hispano herdsman, and developing distinctive
local animals, hybrids of hardy Mexican frontier stock and
blooded imports.

While cattlemen were still moving in upon the open range in
the empty center of the Llano Estacado, the industry was being
rapidly changed into more stable ranching operations. By the
mid-1880's most of the rangeland had been fenced, much of it
had come under the control of large companies supplied with
Eastern and foreign capital, and railroads had replaced the great
cattle trails (Map 12). Railroads were built into this livestock
realm in a pattern similar to the earlier spread of the cattlemen,
with lines reaching out from the Cross Timbers to the Panhandle, across the Rolling Plains, and to the Concho, while out
of South Texas a long line skirted the edge of the Edwards
Plateau and crossed the Trans-Pecos country to El Paso.

Farmers followed slowly in the wake of these advances, principally out the Cross Timbers along the axes of the railroads.
Ranches were broken up and the pastures gave way to grain and
cotton, although livestock remained an important element on
most farms. By 1900 wheat and cotton had reached the base of
the High Plains, and at a dozen places beyond farming had been
or was being tried, although droughts and depressions had
checked any general invasion.

By that date also West Texas was developing a regional consciousness but one as yet rather unfocused. West Texans were
likely to see themselves as part of a simple dualism of West
versus East, their half of the state against all the rest. To some
extent it was a case of rancher versus farmer; more clearly it
was the new versus the old, the frontier versus the metropolis.
Certainly West Texans saw it as a struggle of the politically
weak and neglected against the powerful and privileged; and,
more fundamentally, theirs was a regionalism rooted in basic
environmental and geographical differences which created special local problems and needs. But West Texas was as yet an
area of little coherence. It had been conquered but was only
thinly domesticated and the geographic patterns of its develop-

ment were as yet unstable and uncertain. No sure limit had yet been established to the advance of the farmer, no certain cities had arisen from the many towns competing for regional leadership. It was a sprawling, still relatively empty realm, lying open to land speculators and railroad promoters.

C. NETWORKS

Those railroads which had traversed or tapped West Texas were but elements within an intense, complicated, and momentous struggle for control of the commerce of Texas. Although many companies were involved, geographically it was in general a rivalry between two large networks, one focused upon Galveston Bay and the other upon the core of the nation. Galveston Bay had the headstart and local interests moved vigorously after the war to extend and consolidate their pre-eminence. Houston and Galveston sponsored rival systems of similar intent (Galveston doing so because Houston seasonally imposed an embargo on traffic between the two, ostensibly because of the dangers of yellow fever). By the turn of the century the result was a dense focus of lines between Galveston Bay and the richest and most populous areas of Texas, a more widely extended fan reaching out to Shreveport, the Red River, the Rolling Plains, the Concho, and South Texas, and two much longer lines drawing at least some traffic from far beyond the borders of Texas, one from Los Angeles across southern Arizona and New Mexico to El Paso and San Antonio, and one from Denver and the Colorado Piedmont across the Panhandle Plains (although some of the Colorado trade flowed through New Orleans instead of Galveston) (Map 13). Railroads parallel with the Gulf intersected the feeble efforts of lesser Texas ports to garner anything more than a very local trade. All in all it was an impressive, dominant, and thoroughly Texas-oriented network—but it was challenged at many points.

That the first railroad to arrive at the borders of Texas from out of the North was essentially an iron track upon a cattle trail was an important geographical continuity, for the cattle drives of the late 1860's were the first important commercial links binding Texas directly overland to the booming industrial cen-

ters of the nation. The Missouri, Kansas & Texas Railway built
south from Sedalia, Missouri (the end of the trail for the first
big drive in 1866) and Junction City, Kansas (only twenty
miles east of famed Abilene), crossed the Indian Territory along
the old Texas Trail, and arrived at Colbert's Ferry on the Red
River in 1872, and it was in name and purpose, terminals and
route, but a new manifestation of a recent and revolutionary
pattern. Soon other railroads arrived along other older path-
ways, from St. Louis and Memphis, from Vicksburg and New
Orleans, with Texarkana and Shreveport serving at the portals
where Fulton and Jefferson had before, and they penetrated
and spread into all the regions of Texas as had the immigrants
who had come along these same general routes for half a century or more. The lure of the richest districts brought most of
these lines into focus upon the Black Prairies of North and Central Texas.

Closely bound up with these railroads were others which were
manifestations not so much of older movements as of larger
dreams of continental strategy (Map 13). The Texas & Pacific
was envisioned as a line which would bring trafficways from
the North and the South together in North Texas and unite
them in a trunk line to California, and although it never became
in itself such a transcontinental line it did become part of such
a system. Through its link at Dallas with the St. Louis & San
Francisco it provided a route from Missouri to New Mexico
which was essentially that of the Butterfield stage line of the
1850's. Another line from the northeast corner to San Antonio
and Laredo, cutting across the grain of the Galveston trade, was
geographically akin to, if not exactly along the path of, the axes
of Spanish and Mexican Texas and it represented the vision of
a great new axis of commerce between America and Mexico.
And still another variation of these continental strategies was
the short link to Eagle Pass which was built in anticipation of
an ultimate connection across the breadth of Mexico to the port
of Mazatlan on the Pacific. Shortly after 1900 a similar dream
of connecting Kansas City with Topolobampo actually resulted
in a track across the whole of West Texas from the Red River to
Presidio del Norte. Such lines never achieved their larger pur-

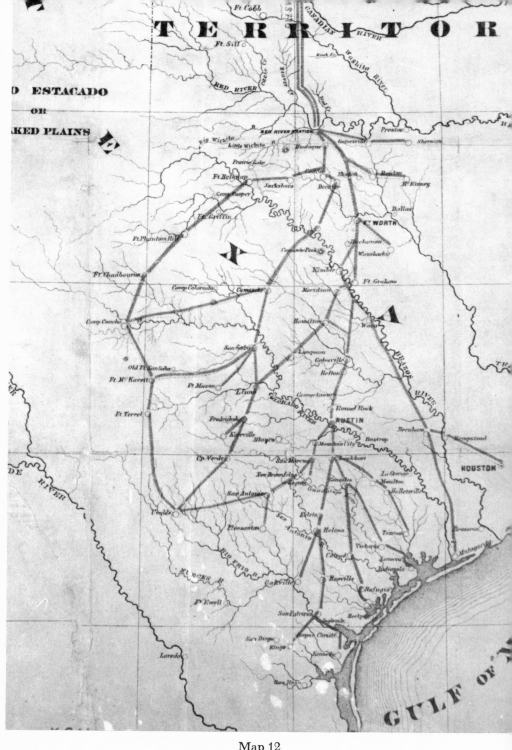

Map 12

"The Best and Shortest Cattle Trail from Texas," Kansas Pacific
Railway [c. 1870].

(Courtesy of the Archives, University of Texas)

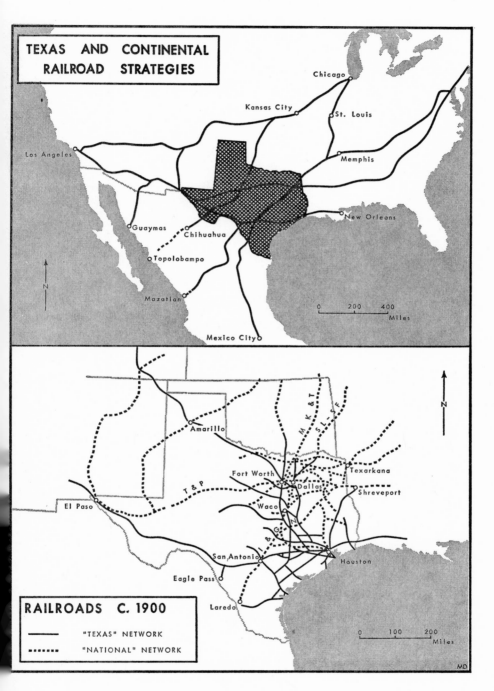

Map 13

poses but they provided valuable service to local districts (and some may yet come closer to their original purpose: the Mexican section of the last-mentioned line was only recently completed, and in 1967 an economic consultant to the Mexican government was in Texas to "generate interest in the movement of traffic to and from the United States through Topolobampo").

It was tempting to Texans to see this entire system of railways, the network within and the lines reaching far beyond her bordering regions to distant centers of commerce, as the very sinews of an empire even greater than ever before envisioned. In the 1890's an eminent geographical survey of the nation described how commerce might well become so channelled by the developing networks of rail and ocean as to make Houston "mistress of an empire," sharing the continent with New York and San Francisco in a logical, tripartite division of Atlantic, Pacific, and Gulf, bringing the whole of the vast "Central belt" into focus upon Buffalo Bayou. It was an exhilarating dream.

D. INVASION

But reality had a different look, for all those strands binding Texas to the American Midlands had been built southward not northward, built into Texas not out from it. Within Texas itself they were everywhere far more competitive than complementary to the local system, designed to divert traffic from rather than feed it to Houston. From the moment the MK&T bridged the Red River produce began to flow northward out of Texas. By 1890 half of the cotton of North Texas went directly by rail to the East rather than by way of Galveston and the sea. But even more significant was the inflow of manufacturers and supplies of all kinds. St. Louis merchants, aided by cheap railroad rates, greater resources, and vigorous promotion, quickly made heavy inroads into the trading territories heretofore complacently controlled by Houston and Galveston. The through cars from Chicago and St. Louis to Houston, which the railroads proudly initiated in the 1880's, served far more to join Texas to the nation than to turn the Midwest to the Gulf.

The impact of this national penetration was felt most directly in North Texas. The whole area was suddenly transformed from a periphery to a threshold. The inflow of new settlers was not large, but the inflow of capital and business, of builders and promoters, quickened the pace and shaped the patterns of development. The old and the new were immediately and vividly exhibited at the very first point of entry. The MK&T arrived in Texas by way of Grayson County and offered to build into Sherman, the county seat, for a relatively modest fee. But Sherman, slumbering about its courthouse square and counting on the arrival of a line from Houston, disdained to pay tribute to this invader from the North. Therefore, in characteristic aggressive Midwestern fashion, the town of Denison was founded a few miles away to become the terminus of the Northern road. Laid out foursquare in an ample but simple grid, named after a Yankee speculator, promoted by an Illinois land agent, and soon full of Irish laborers, Northern businessmen, and St. Louis drummers, Denison was instantly a formidable rival to the older center. For years afterward the two cities self-consciously accentuated their differing origins: "Sherman assumed the pose of an old, established city with Southern ways and cultural resources . . . Sherman prided itself on its schools and society. Denison prided itself on success."

But much the most striking symbol of the impact of these new national connections upon the geography of Texas was the rise of Dallas. For this local trade center of the Grand Prairie rather suddenly became the junction of railroads from North, East, South, and West, a meeting point of all the several strategies. From a town of perhaps 3,000 in 1870, it grew to 10,000 in 1880, and to over 42,000 by 1900. In a widely publicized interview in 1884, Jay Gould, the famed and feared railroad and financial manipulator, likened the advantages of its location to that of Kansas City, predicted a population of 250,000 in fifty years (he was actually a bit short of the mark—Dallas had 260,475 in the census of 1930), and noted that "there is an air of business life and bustle about it that reminds one of a Northern city." It was a telling form of flattery for a city whose life was now so closely intertwined with that of the North.

Dallas, too, had a local rival, but it was not so much a case of the old versus the new, as a case of two regional capitals within

Texas vying to become the principal nexus with the nation. Dallas, emerging as the center of North Texas, had by far the richer region, but Fort Worth, the gateway to and focus of West Texas, served a far larger region and one rapidly developing. To the extent that Texas was an empire reaching beyond its state borders, it now did so principally through Fort Worth: to southwestern Oklahoma, where Greer County, lying between two branches of the Red River, was largely settled and formally claimed by Texas (a dispute settled by the United States Supreme Court in 1896); to Colorado, rather feebly, failing to reorient much of its trade, but nurturing a bond by a useful exchange of Texas lumber for Colorado coal; to New Mexico, where the Pecos Valley was entered first by Texas cattlemen, to be followed by farmers and townsmen, and first tapped by rail from the Texas & Pacific. Yet in none of these areas nor in some parts of Texas itself was its position secure. Though Texans continued to infiltrate into the southern margins of Oklahoma, when that Territory was finally opened, the great land rush was more from its northern than its southern border, and it brought the Middle West suddenly down upon the margins of the earlier Texas encroachment. By 1900 the Atcheson, Topeka, & Santa Fe Railroad had a line from Kansas City right across the Panhandle to Roswell, New Mexico. In Amarillo, where the Texas and the Midwestern lines crossed, commission agents for the Kansas City and Chicago stockyards competed with those from Fort Worth for the cattle trade of a huge realm. And the Panhandle and all these farther borderlands were ambivalent in culture as well as commerce. The first farming community on the Caprock was a Quaker colony from Indiana; one of the first permanent towns in the Panhandle was an Iowa temperance colony, and although Texans followed the railroad northwestward toward Colorado, Midwesterners were soon flooding in along rival lines. Canadian, for example, was very largely a Kansas development, the few Texans being principally those who moved in from by-passed Mobeetie, an old hide-and-cattle town nearby. So, too, Amarillo and Roswell (where the first church, a Methodist Episcopal, South, was part of the West Texas Confer-

ence, centered at San Angelo) were soon swollen by landseekers, businessmen, and promoters from the Midwest. If this was
an empire it was a beleaguered one.

In fact, commercially it made little sense to talk of a Texas
empire. Texas wealth was derived almost entirely from primary
production. Despite many attempts at local packing, most of her
cattle were shipped live to Midwestern markets; she did nothing
with her cotton but gin it and bale it for the textile mills of New
England and Europe; her forests contained enormous amounts
of timber but only in the 1890's did her lumber and shingles
begin to reach the national market, and then as the result of the
work of lumbermen from the Great Lakes who bought up huge
tracts of Texas pine and introduced large-scale operations, an
"influx of northern energy and new methods [which] revolu-
tionized the industry in Texas." "By 1900, the economy of Texas, in terms of the state's leading components, had become integrated thoroughly with that of the rest of the United States on
the colonial basis of supplying raw materials to the industrial-
ized sectors and importing manufactured products."

But "colonial" implied captivity as an entity within a larger
empire, "integrated" did not mean assimilated, and in fact a
strong sense of local identity and independence still pervaded
the state. The authors of the most lengthy and perceptive analysis of the state in the early years of the new century found this
to be at once an obvious and elusive feature. They noted that
Texas was a huge area "somewhat off to herself," because of
her lack of close ties with most of her bordering states, and that
newspapers and public discussions seemed "to direct themselves
more exclusively to the affairs of their own state than seems to
be the case in other states." Texans, in fact, were "prone to regard themselves as . . . different from the rest of the people of
the United States." The authors agreed that Texas was a peculiar amalgam of peoples, for despite the fact that its principal
roots had made it "predominantly Southern in thought and feel-
ing," it was yet very different from the Southeastern states because of the "decidedly Western and cosmopolitan 'feel' " added
by Middlewesterners, Germans, and Mexicans. They did think

that Texans exaggerated their differences from the rest of the nation, and quoted approvingly a "cosmopolitan newcomer" who had remarked that "the only difference between Texans and other people is that they think themselves different." One only wonders if the newcomer stayed long enough to realize just how very important that one difference could be.

Chapter IV

 ELABORATION

~~~~~~

In January, 1901, a wildcat driller struck an enormous pool of oil in a salt dome south of Beaumont. Late in that same year two of the nation's giant meat packing firms each accepted a subsidy from local citizens and agreed to establish large plants in Fort Worth. These two events were in themselves important additions to the Texas economy and they were indicative of the general direction of Texas development in the twentieth century.

A. Oil and Industry

The great gusher at Spindletop was a national sensation, and it was but the first strike in what would be a continuing series of major oil discoveries which would eventually affect nearly every region of Texas. It was of such fundamental importance because it did more than just add oil to the list of primary products and exports: it generated the need for new tools, supplies, and transportation, while local refineries generated the opportunity for an elaborating set of allied industries. Oil thus proved to be a prodigious economic multiplier for Texas. Spindletop's driller was backed by Eastern capitalists and his success started a heavy flow of money into the state; but even more important, that discovery and the many others to follow kept generating great amounts of local wealth, controlled by Texans who in turn invested in Texas. Oil thus created a new rich class,

a new style of life, and a new degree of financial independence
for Texas as a whole, and thus brought a new manifestation of
cultural self-consciousness and commercial imperialism.

The timing and magnitude of Spindletop together with other
nearby discoveries in the next few years, such as the Sour Lake,
Humble, and Goose Creek fields, made the Beaumont-Houston
area a strong focus for the Texas oil industry, and that headstart, continued expansion of local production, and the lure of
shipping and processing facilities have sustained its position
despite major developments in other and often distant regions of
the state. Most of the major producing and processing companies, suppliers, and equipment manufacturers are headquar-
tered in Houston, and the patterns of their operations bind oil
districts far beyond the bounds of Texas in some degree to that
city. Of greatest geographical consequence are the ties thus
made with neighboring states. The oil fields of East Texas, the
Red River Valley and the Panhandle became closely inter-
locked, in companies, commerce, and personnel, with those in
Louisiana and Oklahoma, while in eastern New Mexico the oil
industry, like agriculture, was almost entirely an extension
from Texas of Texas people and patterns.

A great many localities, at least a few in every large region
of Texas, have directly felt the quickening touch of oil. If the
discovery was a major one and not on the fringe of an already
important oil district the social as well as economic impact was
likely to be very great. Towns such as Beaumont, Ranger,
Mexia, Borger, and Kilgore are but the most famous of many
which experienced the tumultuous cycle of an oil boom. Such
communities, large and small, carried the mark of their beginnings long after the boom was past. That explosive growth, the
sudden swirling influx of a heterogeneous crowd of aggressive
rootless people, the feverish speculation, intense competition,
and social disorder, left behind shallow-rooted, fragile communities, lacking in stability and cohesion, alien to their rural surroundings and unrelated to older regional patterns, bound up
with a highly specialized industrial network and stamped in the
image of oil towns everywhere. While new governmental controls and new industrial practices have done much in the last

thirty years to dampen the more frenzied accompaniment of oil discoveries, the new oil town remains a distinctive kind of community, related in people, economy, and society more to others of its type than to older towns of its region untouched by oil.

The Swift and Armour packing plants in Fort Worth marked the direct entry of major national firms lured by local Texas raw materials. Others followed to process other local products of mine, field, and forest, while the ready availability of a variety of fuels—petroleum, natural gas, lignite, Oklahoma coke—led also to the processing of imported materials. Still other companies came primarily to use Texas labor or to assemble and distribute to the growing Texas market. In amongst these national firms a host of local companies dealing with an even wider range of activities also developed. Although in detail it is quite impossible to sort the industries of Texas into simple categories of local and national, it is nevertheless quite appropriate and useful to think of them in such terms. For although the national companies pump much wealth into Texas, they also draw much out, and although local managers may have considerable autonomy, they are ultimately controlled from elsewhere and their activities are but one part of a much wider co-ordinated network. By such firms, Texas as a whole is being made one part of a much larger tightly integrated national economy.

Altogether these developments have transformed Texas from solely a primary producer into a diversified manufacturer, from a "colonial" economy exploited to serve a distant industrial region, to a closely integral part of a national industrial complex. Yet the strong persistence of local as well as national components in this developing economy, the two complexly intertwined yet in some degree contradictory in result, has been an important characterizing feature of twentieth-century Texas. For whereas in most parts of the country, the local, having meager capital resources within itself, has been absorbed or abolished by the national, here, despite the strong domination of the latter, the local component has continued to be sufficiently strong to allow the persistence of an important and recognizable Texas entity within the network of an ever more centralized and uniform American system.

In common with geographical trends elsewhere, this industrial growth has been strongly focused upon well-established commercial centers and thus in general has more reinforced than radically altered older gross regional patterns. An important exception is the Gulf Coast, where chemicals (from a remarkable array of local materials—petroleum, natural gas, salt, sulphur, lime), synthetics, electronics, and an array of other activities have been ramified into a regional industrial complex which not only has given a similarity to but in considerable degree has functionally bound together a lengthy coastal strip from Port Arthur to Corpus Christi.

B. Agriculture and Regions

While oil and industry were profoundly altering the Texas economy, agriculture continued to alter profoundly certain regions. The greatest geographical change of these years was the farmer conquest of the High Plains, a process which brought in several hundred thousand people, produced several considerable towns and cities, and formed two distinct regions in a great block of some forty counties which had been a largely empty and undifferentiated realm of a few big ranches and a few tiny hamlets.

The two regions were importantly different in people and orientation. The conquest of the South Plains was in general but a westward extension of a long established agricultural movement, that variable combination of cotton, grain, and livestock which had been expanding out of the Cross Timbers for half a century. In the face of chronic doubt but with the help of railroads and windmills, new efficient machinery and new hardy plants, this complex found those high desolate flatlands beyond the edge of the Caprock to be its most productive environment. As it was spread to the limits of that environment it was carried beyond the geometrical political boundary to stamp the firm impress of Texas upon a long strip of the borderlands of New Mexico. Although its first railroad ties were north to Amarillo and the Midwest, as agriculture expanded, links with Fort Worth-Dallas and Houston-Galveston were built, and as that agriculture came to be dominated by cotton so these Texas lines came to dominate its traffic, giving to commerce and culture similar regional orientations.

On the other hand, in the Panhandle Plains, north of the Palo Duro, where physical conditions were slightly but critically different, wheat farmers from Kansas, aided by railroads and machinery, new wheats and an enthusiasm for new "dry farming" techniques, brought in an agricultural complex which had been spreading out of the American Midlands for half a century or more. Here the Texas area was but a small political segment of a large farming region, the Winter Wheat Belt, which included much of western Oklahoma and Kansas and eastern Colorado as well, and the whole of which was strongly focused upon Kansas City. Thus differences in environment and crops, people and orientations gave identity to two regions in this part of Texas and made their local capitals, Lubbock and Amarillo, which were so alike in setting, in sudden growth, and now in size, interestingly different cities.

At the other end of Texas another ranching area was being transformed in a very different manner into another distinctive agricultural region. The great boom in the lower Valley of the Rio Grande was in type and time very much akin to similar promotions in Florida, Arizona, and southern California. Railroads and land companies put on a shrill campaign to advertise the fortunes to be made in cities, the certainty of rising land values, the security of a small farm, the amenities of new towns, and the comforts of tropical living. As a result the area was populated and developed more by newcomers from the North than by Texans from nearby; its colonization came not from the southward spread of an existing agricultural pattern but from the implantation of a large enclave into the midst of a ranching region. It was an enclave different in crops but not wholly in people from anything around it, for these new crops required a great deal of field labor and an old source lay ready at hand. Thus this great influx of Anglos into the Valley was accompanied by an even greater influx of Mexicans from across the border, and the old regional pattern of Anglo rancher and Hispano vaqueros was transformed into one of Anglo farmer and foreman and large gangs of Hispano laborers, with a social partitioning of all the many new towns and cities which rapidly grew in this fertile setting. Had the area been settled more directly by Texans spreading west and south along the coastal plain, Negroes would also certainly have been a significant element in the population, whereas they are hardly to be found in the area at all.

Somewhat similarly irrigation and dry farming along the upper Nueces, Frio, and Atascosa made another part of South Texas a productive agricultural district with accompanying social changes. In general this was a more dispersed and less intensive type of development, although in the fertile Winter Garden district around Crystal City and Carrizo Springs the agricultural and social patterns are very like those in the Valley.

These colonizations made Texas unusual in another way for it has been one of the very few parts of the nation to continue to have an expanding agriculture as well as an expanding industry right down to the present. This is not to suggest that Texas agriculture has been everywhere expanding and prosperous, for there are many marginal districts (some in chronic decline) in various stages of difficult readjustment, and there are strong farm-to-city migrations here as elsewhere in the nation. Yet Texas has been sufficiently large, youthful in parts, diversified, wealthy, and dynamic to have sustained an unusually strong over-all rural economy. Thus her population has continued to spread outward over an ever larger proportion of her area while at the same time it was concentrating inward upon a few metropolitan clusters. As a simple indication of this, 93 of the 254 counties had greater populations in 1960 than ever before; that was of course an expression of oil and industry, as well as agriculture, and even in farming areas most of the increase was in the smaller cities rather than in the countryside; yet over-all, Texas had an areal pattern of growth which was unusually widespread for mid-twentieth-century America.

C. POPULATION AND CULTURE

Altogether that pattern included nearly ten million people, a result of a rate of increase in every decade greater than that of the United States as a whole. It was a growth which continued to be sustained by very considerable immigration from other states (although in some years the number of Texans moving to Oklahoma, New Mexico, and other western states was greater than the number coming in). Although no comprehensive analyses have been made, it appears that that inflow has been in general similar in sources and patterns to those of the last century, with perhaps some increase in the proportion from the Upper South and the North.

Census data do clearly distinguish two of the ethnic components of the population, the Negro and the Hispano (the latter figures based upon a large sample of surnames). The first are a gradually decreasing proportion of the total (12.6 percent in 1960), the second a gradually increasing proportion (14.8 percent in 1960), and each remains very important in the social geography of several regions. Although both still live mainly in those areas where their roots are deepest, they have also spread into some newer districts, especially into the cotton and oil areas of West Texas (Map 14). The other major culture group, the Europeans, are no longer readily distinguished in the census and that fact is of course but a reflection of their recession as a cultural entity. After the 1920's those groups which had maintained a rather clear cultural identity to that time were no longer significantly reinforced by new immigrants and thus the passing of time began to weaken their European ties precisely as new instruments of communication and mobility began to strengthen the many influences toward assimilation. Nevertheless, although virtually all are now English in speech not all are as yet "Anglo" in culture, for in such matters as religion and politics, local society and cultural values, they still give an important distinctiveness to certain Texas areas.

Perhaps most remarkable of all among the general developments of these years was the fact that despite the manifold relentless forces of national integration and homogenization, Texans continued to regard themselves and to be regarded by others as a people with a difference, Americans of a special breed. Unlike so many characterizations of regional cultures in America, the popular concept of the Texan as a type is more than an innocuous caricature rooted in an archaic folklore, more than local

color sustained by regional advertising; it is a concept which still
has vitality and meaning in the daily lives of people. That it
does so is because the original elements of the tradition were
well rooted in the early special experiences of Texan people and
these elements have been recurrently strengthened and newer
elements successfully grafted on during the whole subsequent
course of Texan development. In the perspective of a century
and a half of Anglo-Texas some of the main features and factors
of that tradition can be reasonably well identified.

The early popular image of the "Typical Texan" clearly
arose out of the frontier; he was from the first a special variant
of a general type: the Kentuckian writ large, Daniel Boone
loosed upon a larger arena, the rugged, self-reliant, adventurous
frontiersman—mobile, aggressive, and adaptive, glorying in the
challenge of the wilderness. It was an image not only exaggerated to fit the size of Texas but exaggerated, clarified, and crys-
tallized by the encounter with an alien people of very different
type. The sharp contrast, conflict, suffering, and triumph which
marked the Texan's relations with Mexicans was in general not
unlike the experiences along the whole American frontier between the Anglos and the Indians, but here it was magnified
into an intensely focused, vital, bloody encounter between civilized peoples. That the frontiersmen of Texas by themselves defeated the Mexican state could not but foster an unusual pride
and assurance of inherent superiority, and a decade of political
independence born of such travail and possessed of such an ex-
panse could not but foster a chauvinistic vision of the realities
and potentialities of Texas. The very existence of the Republic
of Texas of course gave to the area and its people a unique identity, unavoidably acknowledged by all Americans, and when the
smaller republic joined the larger it did so sufficiently on its own
terms as to perpetuate that identity in law as well as in mind;
Texas simply is not, in fact, just another state, as neither Texan
nor national officials are ever allowed to forget.

All of these experiences reinforced Texan self-reliance as well
as self-consciousness, and here again was a common frontier
trait unusually sustained by the prolonged existence of frontier
conditions—prolonged not so much by any slowness of develop-

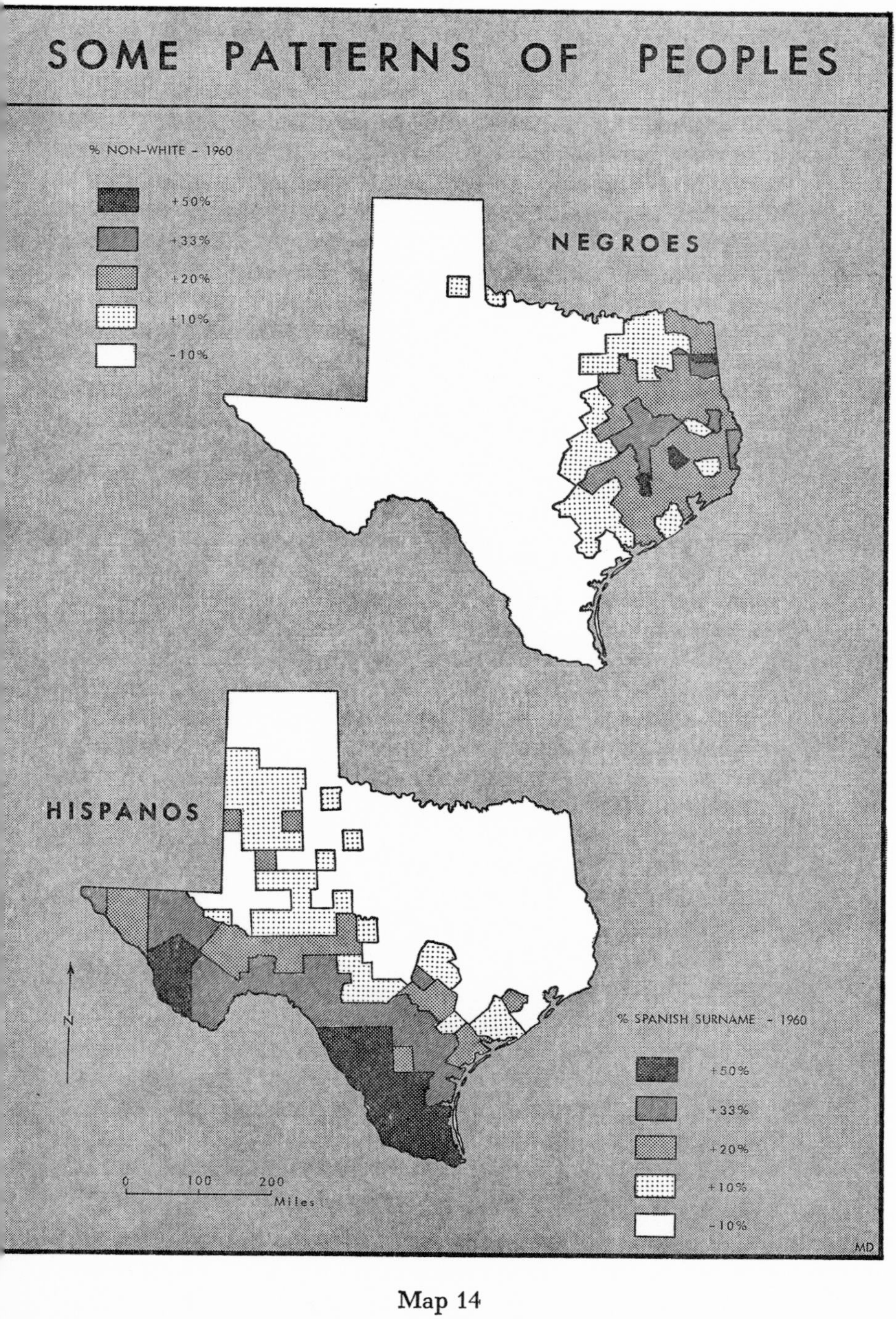

SOME PATTERNS OF PEOPLES

% NON-WHITE - 1960

+50%
+33%
+20%
+10%
-10%

NEGROES

HISPANOS

% SPANISH SURNAME - 1960

+50%
+33%
+20%
+10%
-10%

N

0   100   200
          Miles

MD

Map 14

ment as by the great size and variety of the area to be developed. Agricultural colonization, the implanting of new homes in new lands, went on continuously on a major scale in Texas from the 1820's through the 1920's, a span unequalled in any other region of Anglo-America. The most famous part of that expansion, however, was that of the cowboy rather than the farmer. Thus the Typical Texan was gradually altered in the popular image to become the frontiersman on horseback and instead of fading into a folk memory as the farmers conquered the range, or merely being speciously perpetuated in the romanticism of the popular arts, he evolved into the successful rancher, secure on lands unsuited to the plow and secure in the popular mind as a prestigious symbol of the good life.

Because Texas has expanded over so long a time and so large an area, land speculation has been a persistent feature of Texas life, and it has been magnified by the fact that control of public lands has rested in Austin rather than Washington, and by the hazards of nature and of the market, especially in West Texas and especially where ranching and farming were done on such a large scale. But such endemic instabilities were mild compared to the prodigious speculative possibilities inherent in oil. With oil the prospect of riches was ever before the poorest Texan, for the means of attainment could as easily be blind luck or a wild gamble as the industrious use of unusual talents. The widespread occurrence of oil in Texas made it difficult to regard land as anything but a form of speculative capital, and although that might seem an ugly distortion of the older American agrarian dream it was by no means alien to the tradition of the restless Southern frontiersman (nor in fact to his more commercially minded Northern brother) who sat lightly upon his land, ever ready to abandon one locality for another in hopes of better country or better luck. Thus oil was readily infused into the veins of the Typical Texan and added enormous wealth to the list of personal features which were regarded as descriptive of the type. That the Typical Texan became either the rancher who struck it rich in oil on his own land, or the parvenu oilman who immediately invested in ranches and cattle is convincing evidence of the continuity in this Texan type; it is the evolution of a single tradition, rather than the competition of an old and a new.

The Typical Texan is of course a caricature, an exaggeration of a few features among many, of the more peculiar instead of the more common, but it is of interest because it is rooted in some realities and because it is the popular way of emphasizing the fact that Texans are regarded as a special type within American culture. It is basically sound, but romanticized and incomplete.

The basic soundness of the caricature is confirmed by the studies of social scientists who have carefully examined Texas communities in a search for dominant traits and social patterns. Such researchers would be quite uncomfortable with the very idea of a Typical Texan, but their studies clearly reveal that some characteristics are so common that we may continue for the moment to use the term. The Texan emerges from these investigations as one who is strongly individualistic and egalitarian, optimistic and utilitarian, volatile and chauvinistic, ethnocentric and provincial, as one still very much under the influence of older rural and moral traditions. Such a person regards government as no more than a necessary evil, distrusts even informal social action as a threat to his independence, and accepts violence as an appropriate solution to certain kinds of personal and group problems. Material wealth is much admired for its own sake but industriousness has no particular virtue; land has prestige, but especially in the form of the ranch or the plantation, for cattle and cotton have symbolic value while manual field work should be left to Negroes. Thus the security of the small family farm ranks very low on the scale of values. There is an easy acceptance of equality among one's own kind but a rigid sense of superiority over other local peoples, and a deep suspicion of outsiders as threats to the social order. The narrow moral strictures of Protestant fundamentalism are accepted as an ideal moral code but certain covert violations are routinely tolerated (such as the use of hard liquor).

A community of such persons obviously exhibits a similar image and expectedly the Texas town tends to be rather loosely organized, weak in formal government and in civic co-operation. Church and family are the central institutions but neither of these has a strong cohesion: the one is as likely as the other to be factionalized by personal differences, leading to splinter sects and family feuds, despite long neighborly associations and widespread kinship networks. So strong and pervasive is the emphasis upon personal freedom that sociologists have labelled it an atomistic social order. It is also a hierarchical order, with the more wealthy landowners and businessmen at the top, small white proprietors and white workers ranged in the middle, and Negroes and Hispanos of whatever occupation at the bottom. It is basically a white, Anglo-Saxon, fundamentalist-Protestant society, in which other religious groups are regarded as somewhat anomalous, even though in some cases entirely respected, and other racial groups are regarded as natural adjuncts, to be firmly locked into patterns of residential segregation, social discrimination, political subservience, and economic dependence.

No one of these individual traits or community features is in itself peculiar to Texas; it is only the proportionate emphasis which differentiates this regional manifestation from the national—a generalization which supports the underlying theme of John Bainbridge's impertinent but penetrating book *The Superamericans*, wherein the peculiarities in behavior of certain kinds of wealthy Texans are seen as but exaggerations of some common American traits. Viewed more closely, these Texas patterns of attitude and behavior clearly reflect their Southern source regions and could be loosely generalized to fit nearly the whole Southeastern quadrant of the nation. Yet, in detail, the Texas pattern does emerge as different; different in its special emphasis of otherwise common features, in its special relationship with Hispanic peoples, in its incorporation of the complex influences of ranching and oil, and, above all, in its insistent self-conscious pride in Texas. Texas is, in short, an American region, Southern in source, Southwestern in locale, but definitely Texan in character.

Chapter V

★ DIFFERENTIATION

〜〜〜〜〜〜〜〜〜〜〜〜〜〜〜〜〜〜〜〜〜〜〜〜〜〜〜

ALTHOUGH EVEN SUCH A BRIEF CHARACTERIZATION HELPS IN a gross way to differentiate Texas from its surroundings, it does not effectively describe Texas as a culture area for it suggests a uniformity which could not possibly exist over so large and varied a country. It is a characterization which ignores a quarter of the people of Texas, other than describing where they fit as captives in a social hierarchy, and glosses over important differences among the other three quarters. It epitomizes an influence which pervades the whole but is itself complexly varied from place to place, reflecting differences in social heritage, physical environment, economic activities, and proportions of peoples. Unfortunately it is impossible to measure and to map such variations in detail. Lacking a census of social attitudes and community structure, the social geography of Texas must be based upon a few general indicators, a few special studies, and an uneven miscellany of information and impressions. The most useful of the comprehensive data are the federal census figures on Negro and Hispano distributions, the private census (1952) figures on church denominations and memberships, and the regular recurrent results of political elections. From the patterns and proportions revealed by such county data some reasonable inferences about social structure and values can certainly be made and when combined with an historical perspective on the movements of peoples into the various districts, the patterns of

their economic activities, and their geographic orientations, at
least a crude approximation of the regional cultural geography
of Texas is possible (Map 15). However insufficient the means
the end is sufficiently important to warrant the try.

A. EAST TEXAS

From the very beginning of Texas the Eastern Timbers country, the rolling red hills and piney woods east of the Trinity,
has been routinely regarded as a distinct region; and despite
some significant new patterns and a somewhat lessened importance to the whole, it still is. And it is so, simply because those
patterns of society which began to give it regional identity well
over a century ago are still so pervasive as to preserve its integrity. In its rural areas it is still essentially the western extension of the Old South, a stable bi-racial society, conservative and
fundamentalist, provincial and poor. Cotton, once the sole money
crop of the northern half of the region, is gone from the scene,
but the scars of the chronic decline that preceded its disappearance are still very much in evidence: gullied fields gone to waste
and impoverished people barely touching the margins of modern
society. Corn, hogs, and poultry, electricity, tractors, and trucks
have been the means of renewal, but average acreages remain
small and average densities remain high despite a continual migration outward to other regions.

Here Anglo and Negro form a society which is at once bi-
racial and homogeneous, segregated and cohesive, the two locked
together in a century-old relationship. Negroes make up more
than a quarter of the regional population—a half in some counties and far more in many rural districts—but they are everywhere amongst a white population of old Southern country
stock, undiluted by Europeans, Hispanos, or newcomers from
the North, undisturbed by radical urban and industrial changes,
and thus they very largely remain a pliant submissive mass
within a stable paternalistic hierarchy unshaken by radical
social and political movements. Despite white and black, the
society is a homogeneous one, for the daily life and the world
view of both are strongly shaped by the same code, a powerful,
deep-rooted Southern fundamentalism. Baptists, Methodists, and

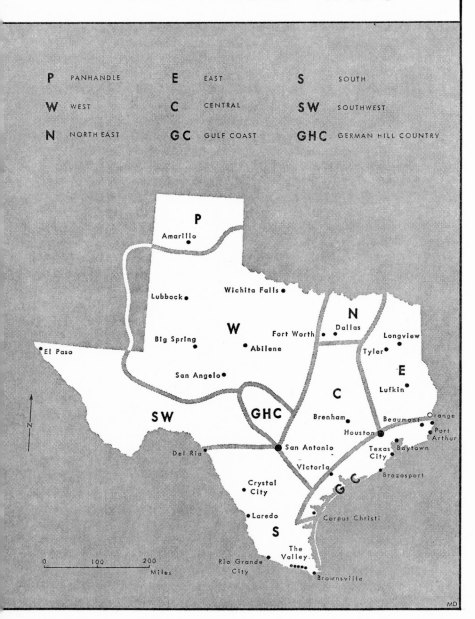

CULTURE AREAS 1960'S

P PANHANDLE   E EAST   S SOUTH

W WEST   C CENTRAL   SW SOUTHWEST

N NORTH EAST   GC GULF COAST   GHC GERMAN HILL COUNTRY

P
Amarillo

Lubbock
Wichita Falls
N
Dallas
W
Fort Worth
Longview
Big Spring
Tyler
El Paso
Abilene
E
San Angelo
Lufkin

SW
GHC
C
Brenham
Beaumont
Orange
Houston
Port Arthur
Del Rio
San Antonio
Texas City
Baytown
Victoria
Brazosport
GC
Crystal City
Laredo
Corpus Christi
S
The Valley
Rio Grande City
Brownsville

N

0   100   200
Miles

MD

Map 15

various pentecostal sects almost monopolize the religious scene
—Lutherans are virtually unknown, Episcopalians an old but
tiny minority, Roman Catholics a small and suspect one (in Nacogdoches descendants of the earliest Catholic settlers of Spanish
and Mexican days retain their identity primarily through their
religion).

It is typical of Texas that the main intrusion upon these older
patterns has come from oil. The great East Texas field created
Kilgore and transformed such towns as Longview and Tyler into
prosperous small cities in the 1930's; and the Lone Star steel
works, a modern success after numerous earlier failures to make
use of local ores, broadened the industrial base in the 1940's, so
that a swath of thriving industrial centers has developed along
the Dallas-Shreveport axis across the northern half of the region. Such communities, as well as a few others here and there,
such as Lufkin, the lumber, pulp, and paper center of the piney
woods, obviously have a form of economy and a level of prosperity unknown in the general countryside. Although still
rather new and anomalous their steadily enlarging and expanding influence is gradually remolding the whole region more and
more into their own image.

But an even much more urban and industrial East Texas will
probably not be radically different from the old, for so far it
has remained a region of the same people. Its modern towns and
cities are local growths, gatherings from the countryside, a
minor spatial change of little immediate consequence to the relations of black and white or to basic social mores. Even the
impact of oil was softened by the ready supply of labor at hand
and the fact that the non-Texans attracted came very largely
from immediately adjacent states of similar culture. The fact
that more Anglos than Negroes have migrated to local cities has
modified local racial proportions without softening local racial
relations. Such changes have, however, undermined some of the
solidarity of the East Texas political bloc (Goldwater carried two
of the industrial counties in 1964).

East Texas is therefore a combination of economic change and
social continuity, a region marked by the slow evolution of a

single, solid, deep-rooted tradition. It is a region where rural ways still shape urban life, a society which is only gradually opening itself to a wider world, only grudgingly yielding to external pressures. It is a region in which the "Negro question" remains the transcendant political issue, in which temperance and tobacco, card playing and evolution can still be lively social concerns, and where rural unemployment continues as a chronic economic problem. With the plantation long gone and the ranch never appropriate it is the one area of Texas in which land seems more a heavy burden than a means of wealth, more the seat of poverty than a source of prestige. Now much weakened in power and influence and much less typical in cultural patterns this oldest province is, nevertheless, no less distinctive a part of the Texas empire than it was a century ago.

B. The Gulf Coast

East Texas is, however, rather less inclusive than before because the lower Sabine-Neches corner is now more closely bound to and comparable with other coastal developments than with the interior. Beaumont-Port Arthur-Orange is but one of a series of important interrelated clusters along the Gulf from Sabine Pass to Corpus Christi which have made that lengthy portion of the coast a distinctive region. Its emergence is wholly a twentieth-century phenomenon, and its present form is very recent. The flat wet prairies and the shallow sheltered bays and lagoons of the Coastal Plain are an obviously distinct physical region, but it was long a swampy and unhealthful one, and was only sparsely occupied, chiefly along its rivers and better bays in a series of small settlements, each group serving a separate interior district. The earlier development of larger cities did not in itself alter this basic geography, for these too were simply expressions of developing hinterlands. It was Spindletop that initiated a new pattern. Within a very few years oil had created many new centers and industries, and the areas bordering and between Sabine Lake and Galveston Bay were knit together by a network of pipelines, railroads, and coastal shipping. Subsequent oil discoveries westward along the Coastal Plain ex-

tended that network and type of development. It is only, however, in the last twenty-five years with the rapid elaboration
of an enormous, complex chemical industry and related facilities that economic and social patterns have emerged in such
forms as to stamp the entire area as a distinctive human region.

Geographically it is still a series of clusters, but now with
much larger developments more closely spaced and regionally
interdependent. The plain is laced with pipelines and an enormous traffic moves laterally along this coast, by sea or by the
Intracoastal Canal. Refineries and a great array of other processing plants are not only grouped around major ports but spotted
through every district, sometimes looming starkly out of a flat
vacant countryside. As a consequence of the dispersed pattern of
this development every county of the region has grown in population and many have more than doubled in the past twenty
years. The greatest amount of growth has come to the older and
larger cities—Beaumont, Port Arthur, Houston, Victoria, Corpus Christi—but proportionate increase has been much greater
in a dozen smaller centers. Whole new sprawling, loosely articulated urban complexes—Texas City, Baytown, Brazosport—
have appeared almost suddenly, and because of the ease of long
distance commuting over the fine roads across the flat plain
former crossroads hamlets have been swollen by subdivisions,
trailer parks, and roadside shopping centers.

Unlike East Texas, these communities are not primarily local
growths, fed by a redundant rural population, for such numbers
have never lived in this countryside. The towns may be old in
name but they are not only new in growth and appearance but
full of people new to the region. Probably most of these people
are not new to Texas, but the proportion of those from other
states is larger here than in any other major region. Many of
these, as elsewhere in Texas, are from Louisiana, Arkansas, and
Oklahoma, but, again, the proportion from the North is also
greater here than elsewhere. Furthermore, because the industries are highly technical and mostly controlled by national
firms, the Northerners are especially prominent at the higher
economic levels. They are also a group which is continually

San Antonio de Bexar, as sketched by Herman Lungkwitz, who came to New aunfels in 1850. "The domes and white clustered dwellings . . . basking in the ge of a vast plain" (Olmsted) are apparent, although the rather lush Germanic atment of trees and clouds has softened the harshness and brilliance of the South xas landscape.

(Courtesy of the Barker Library, The University of Texas)

2. The composite architecture of San Antonio—Mexican adobe, American Greek revival, and German low hip roof—in an old view of Market Street.

3. The focus of the Texas hinterland: cotton, wood products, and boxcar merchandise at the junction of rail and water—Buffalo Bayou at the foot of Main Street, Houston, in 1867.

The link with a wider world: sidewheel steamers offering scheduled service to New Orleans and New York at the Morgan Pier, Galveston, 1861.

(Courtesy of the Rosenberg Library, Galveston)

5. A Texas trail herd, watering on the San Saba River, en route to stock the Llano Estacado, 1887.
(Courtesy of the N. H. Rose Collection, University of Oklahoma Library)

6.   Wool wagons at Sonora, on the Edwards Plateau, 1898.
(Courtesy of the N. H. Rose Collection, University of Oklahoma Library)

7.   A "bird's-eye" view of Quanah, 1890. Finding itself off the route of the Fort Worth & Denver City, the hamlet of Quanah voted to relocate; lot sales were opened at the new site on December 1, 1886. This stylized depiction of the results four years later no doubt exaggerates the starkness of the scene, but it well portrays a Texas example of a broader phenomenon: the almost instantaneous conquest of the prairies in an almost invariable civic pattern, a rigid gridiron of streets centered upon the railroad track, lined by white boxlike houses and struggling shade trees.

(Courtesy of the Barker Library, The University of Texas)

8.   The wealth of Wichita Falls, 1900: wheat from Archer and Young counties awaiting buyers on a street lined with fine façades of brick and stone.

(Courtesy of the N. H. Rose Collection, University of Oklahoma Library)

9. The Gulf Coast. Refineries on the stark coastal plain, the chief landscape symbol of the new industrial Texas.

(Courtesy of the Texas Highway Department)

10. South Texas. Harlingen, laid out foursquare but curiously discordant with the railroad whose construction prompted its birth in 1905, is now the largest of the many new towns which were products of the intensive Anglo development of the subtropical lower Rio Grande Valley, and it well reflects the vigorous modern growth of this major bicultural subregion.

(Courtesy of the Lower Rio Grande Valley Chamber of Commerce)

11. The Hill Country. A Roman Catholic church and rectory in the hilly brush-lands of German Texas. The mottled fieldstone and metal roof, front veranda, and boxlike shape are typical of an old tradition in local architecture.

(Photo by the author)

12. Southwest Texas. El Paso, attenuated between the barren shoulder of Franklin Mountain and the sandy bed of the Rio Grande, the great imperial outpost serving New Mexico (far background) and beyond, and together with its Mexican twin, Ciudad Juarez (lower third of the photo), the largest Anglo-Hispano binational metropolis.

(Courtesy of the El Paso Chamber of Commerce)

13.   Central Texas. Gonzales, an Anglo town in a Hispano frame, laid out by a M
sourian according to explicit Mexican directives: a gridiron set to the cardinal dire
tions with a central cluster of five public squares. Today the county courthouse a
jail occupy the center square, those to the north (left) and west (foreground) rema
largely open plazas (the former contains the fire station), those to the east and sou
(beyond the edge of this photo) are dominated by churches (Methodist and Bapt
on the former, Presbyterian on the latter).

Central Texas. Lockhart, seat of Caldwell County, directly north of Gonzales
unty, displays a more common Texas pattern: the single courthouse square sur-
nded by business frontages which shield the shopper from the subtropical sun and
n by broad continuous awnings, an elemental plan whose lineage very likely
ds back to Middle Tennessee.

(Courtesy of Frank B. Whaley)

15.   Central Texas. The large Church of the Annunciation towering over the little village of St. Hedwig is a bold exhibit of the deep-rooted and strongly expressed cultural variety of the region. Founded in the 1850's, the village is one of several Polish communities in the country southeast of San Antonio.
(Courtesy of the Chancery Office, Archdiocese of San Antonio)

The Core. Austin as a seat of power: the state government, focused on the capi-
(center), and the state university, focused on the Memorial Tower of the library
per left center). Founded at what was considered a strategic site along the con-
t of the eastern lowlands with the western highlands (the hills begin just beyond
left edge of this photo), its main strategic advantage today accrues from its posi-
n on the thoroughfares between Dallas and San Antonio (note Interstate 35 cut-
g across the upper right).

(Courtesy of the Texas Highway Department)

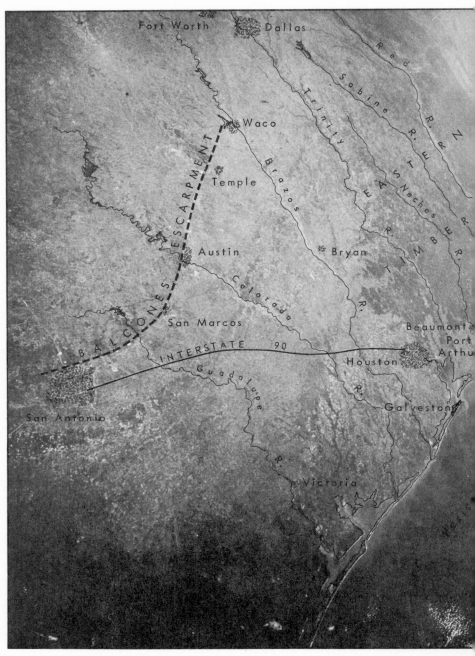

17. The entire core of Texas in a single spectacular view from Gemini XII, November 14, 1966.

(Courtesy National Aeronautics and Space Administration, Houston)

changing in persons, for many are here on assignment as managers, scientists, engineers, or special technicians who can expect to be reassigned eventually to other plants in other parts of the nation or the world.

Obviously, such non-indigenous, dynamic communities have little in common with even the largest and most progressive cities of East Texas. The much greater mixture of peoples new to the area has necessarily resulted in a much more flexible social patterning among them. Here the hierarchy is not dominated by old families and structured around landowner and tenant, or even factory owner and laborer; rather, it is dominated by local families of new wealth and new families who are local directors of national firms. Social structure will tend to be a hierarchy of managers and technicians, research directors and research assistants, all of whom will be more likely to spend their weekends fishing on the Gulf than visiting kinfolk in the back country. There are both Negroes and Hispanos in the lower levels of this looser social order, their proportions differing considerably from one end of the region to another. Negroes make up about a fifth of the population east of Matagorda but only 5 to 10 percent west to Corpus Christi, while conversely the Hispanos make a fifth or even much more on the western end, 8 to 10 percent in the middle, and only 2 to 3 percent east of Galveston Bay. These patterns reflect recent westward and eastward migrations, respectively, of the two groups and also some rather dense rural populations in a few areas of intensive agriculture. Although neither people are granted social equality by the Anglos, the whole character of regional development fosters a somewhat less rigid pattern of discrimination.

The variety of religious denominations is another simple clue to differences between East Texas and the Gulf. Baptists and Methodists are dominant in the region as a whole, but Roman Catholics, Lutherans, Episcopalians, and Presbyterians have churches in nearly every county and the Catholics are much the largest church from Refugio west. And a mere list masks further variety, for there are Irish (some of whom are descendants of the earliest colonists), German, Czech, and Anglo Roman Catho-

lics as well as Hispano; and the cosmopolitan Southern Baptist
urban congregation is certainly a very different sociological
group from that of the country preacher and his followers.

This Coastal Plain is prospering in agriculture as well as
industry, and to a considerable degree the one is dependent upon
and in some ways similar to the other. For it is a land of large
ranches and plantations, capitalist enterprises devoted to cattle,
cotton, and rice controlled by wealthy oil men and industrial-
ists. Thus even some of the country towns are dominated more
by managers and foremen than by local landowners. In the
western counties of the region there are numerous Germans,
Czechs, Italians, and Midwesterners on smaller farms, a rural
society much more akin to that just to the north than to the rest
of the Gulf Coast and an obvious example of how regional
bounds based upon some dominant set of characteristics (industrial and urban) can be discordant with those based upon others
(agricultural and rural).

Certainly on the whole this Gulf Coast is more generally and
closely a part of the urban-industrial world than any other region of Texas, and it is increasingly becoming popularly recognized as a distinct region. Politically, for example, although in
some ways a strongly conservative region it is so more in a
modern ideological sense than in the traditional provincial sense
found in East Texas; and the realities of its industrial and social
structure have at the same time made it the least anti-labor region in a strongly anti-labor state. It is a new, still emergent
region, a vital part of the new empire, obviously yet not typ-
ically Texan.

C. South Texas

South Texas has been regarded as a distinct and major region
from the moment Texan authority was firmly established anywhere beyond the Nueces. Today in these warm sandy plains,
as in so many parts of Texas, the stockman shares the scene
with the farmer and, in about half the counties, with the oilman.
Along the nothern margins dryland farming is now established
well beyond what was long considered the natural boundary
between cropland and rangeland, but elsewhere cultivation is

exactly circumscribed by the spread of water upon the land and large ranches and intensive oases are most characteristic.

But of course South Texas has persisted as a region more especially because of more important human patterns. It is the great stronghold of the Hispanos. Captured, harassed, deprived, but never expelled they are present today in larger numbers than ever before, constituting a majority in the region as a whole, and three quarters or more of the total in half a dozen counties. Instead of gradually pushing the Hispano back, confining him to a steadily narrowing border zone, every Anglo development has brought a positive Hispano response, the immigration of the one matching that of the other, and just as most of the Anglos have been here no more than a generation or two, so most of the Hispanos have crossed the Rio Grande during that same time.

In general South Texas is everywhere a bi-cultural region, two peoples economically interdependent but socially segregated. Wherever there are large numbers of each, there are two complete societies side by side, each with its homes, shops, churches, schools, newspapers, and social facilities. But there are important differences from place to place in proportions and situations. Where the Anglos are a small minority and have been long established, the two peoples may be well integrated, as in Rio Grande City with its few Anglo merchants, or, on a much larger scale, in Laredo where the international trade and traffic supports a large Hispano as well as Anglo commercial group. In such places there is an easy intermingling among the commercial and professional classes of the two cultures, much bi-lingualism on both sides, and even considerable intermarriage. But much more common are the dual towns, wherein the two peoples are sharply segregated under Anglo political and economic dominance; in smaller settlements where the Hispanos are almost entirely farm laborers, the result can more accurately be called an Anglo town with an Hispano slum.

It is in the great oasis, the broad lower Rio Grande Valley—locally simply "the Valley"—where this Anglo-Hispano relationship is most intense and portentous, a situation arising out of the scale and special origins of the confrontation. The sudden

Anglo invasion of the 1920's came in upon the most complete
and undisturbed Hispano society in Texas. Deep-rooted and
stable even despite its loss of control over much of its land, it
was still essentially an extension of Mexico, linked by trade and
traffic, schools, societies, and newspapers, kinfolk and friends to
nearby regions south of the river. The Anglo conquest was a
shock but not a shattering one; although automatically relegated to an inferior social status, the Hispanos were sufficiently
numerous and possessed the facilities, pride, and vitality to provide a strong nucleus around which the steady stream of Mexican immigrants could form; and the whole could stoutly resist
assimilation.

Although the majority of the incoming Anglos were from the
Middle West they readily adopted the standard Texan (one
could almost say standard American) pattern of superiority over
a non-Anglo laboring class. In other respects, however, they established a society which was not so typical of Texas. Most were
from towns and smaller cities, business and professional men already well detached from rural roots, who were lured by land as
an investment. Such a mélange of newcomers, undominated by
Southern fundamentalism, inevitably established a more flexible, progressive, open society. Such a pattern was also fostered
by the method and timing of colonization—a great land boom
of intensely competitive promotions during the new automobile
age. The result was a blurring of rural-urban distinctions and
the initiation of what would become an almost continuous urban
strip, a "Main Street" of the Valley, seventy miles long, thread-
ing a dozen corporate communities.

In these instant towns the spatial separation of Anglo and
Hispano was a formal part of the original design, a Little Mexico
on one side of the tracks as a natural counterpart of the Anglo-
American community on the other, and the two have lived with
only minimal contact ever since. Many Hispanos work on the
Anglo side but only a very few live there and those who do run
the heavy risk of being ostracized by both sides, the poignant
price of integration wherever two societies exist in such cultural
tension.

Tension is very real and persistent if not always overt and

severe. In such dual towns any social action on the one side is watched uneasily on the other, for each has reason to fear that social change might be forced upon it. While the Hispanos face chronic social and economic pressures from the Anglo, the Anglo is ever faced with the latent political power of a Hispano majority. That power has already been demonstrated in a few places (first of all, in 1963, in Crystal City in the Winter Garden district) and the implications have reverberated throughout South Texas. In such a context Anglo resistance to labor organizers is much less a concern for the costs of production than for the costs of social and political change. Such tensions of culture contact are expressed most intensely in the larger oases of South Texas and are the most definitive characteristic of its social geography.

D. SOUTHWEST TEXAS

Anglo and Hispano also share the rest of a broad Mexican border zone which includes part of the Edwards Plateau and nearly all of the Trans-Pecos, but in a pattern sufficiently simpler to warrant separate regional identification as Southwest Texas. With no oil, only a few very small oases, and no industrial or agricultural prospects for expansion, it has remained from the time the two entered together in the wake of the Apaches the land primarily of Anglo ranchers and Hispano cowboys and herders. The Hispanos are a large minority, augmented by the seasonal migrations of shearing crews coming up onto the Plateau from such places as Uvalde and Del Rio. The towns are ranch supply centers, county seats, railroad or highway service centers, bi-cultural, but mostly in the pattern of an Anglo town with an Hispano slum somewhere down along the tracks. Both peoples are spread thinly over the land, and the Hispanos, lacking either the numbers or the leadership of those in South Texas, remain socially stagnant and politically inert.

El Paso and its environs is an interesting exception to the more general regional pattern. In some ways it seems a western counterpart of the lower end of the Valley: the city poised—like Brownsville—on the border opposite its Mexican twin, an old Anglo fort and frontier outpost in Hispano country, backed by an irrigated oasis. But there are also important differences in scale and character. The city is much larger and the oasis much smaller in this far western corner and in neither was the Anglo entry a sudden invasion. Even the early Hispano beginnings are interestingly different, for settlement began here as a refuge for the Spanish and the Christian Indians driven out of New Mexico in 1680 by the Pueblo revolt. Under Anglo leadership El Paso has developed for a hundred years as the commercial capital of an extensive region largely beyond the limits of Texas. While it has much in common with Brownsville and, more especially, with Laredo, its history and population, industries and commerce, make it more New Mexican in type and function than Texan, and it thus stands as a kind of outpost of empire, in many ways more attached to the country beyond than to that of its political ties.

E. THE GERMAN HILL COUNTRY

The German area of the Hill Country persists as a cultural anomaly on the borderlands of West Texas. It is a compact block of half a dozen counties centered upon Fredericksburg, approximating the area staked out by German colonists over a century ago. It remains a distinctive region because of the success of those early colonists and their descendants in making a living out of a marginally productive country, because they have maintained a strong social cohesion and local identity, and because there has been no oil or other source of wealth to attract other people into the area.

It is a farming and ranching country, specializing on mohair production, a rough rolling wooded and brushy landscape in which here and there a steep-roofed cabin of buff and brown field stone still displays an old distinctively German imprint. The Germans of the area today are thoroughly "Americanized," no longer so easily identified by language and dress, but are still a relatively homogeneous group, conscious of their identity and bound together by a long tradition. German Methodist, Lutheran, and Roman Catholic churches dominate the region. These counties are also a political region, an old Republican stronghold, returning majorities in some years, large minorities in others; they are also traditionally wet in temperance legislation. It is an area of very few Negroes, and of markedly fewer Hispanos than counties to the south and west. There are of course even more Germans to the east but in Central Texas they are but one element in the most heterogeneous culture area of the state, while those Germans who have moved north and west from this Hill Country have settled amongst and largely blended in with the predominant Anglo population. Thus the original area has persisted with little expansion or contraction, a "culture island" unusual in size and homogeneity.

F. West Texas

The term "West Texas" is varied in usage and usually vague in definition, and as a concept in cultural geography it certainly cannot be given precise definition in character or limits. It may in general be applied to a broad region from the Western Cross Timbers to the Pecos Valley, lying approximately between the Red River on the north and the Concho on the south. Physically it includes several belts of complexly dissected lower plains, the broad elevated flat block of the Southern High Plains, and fringes of the Edwards Plateau. It is a region of farms and ranches. On the eastern side farmland is scattered and the farms are smaller and diversified, farther west in small basins of level fertile soils cotton is dominant, while up on the High Plains irrigated cotton and grain sorghums form the main basis of a large and very productive agricultural region. Ranching is found wherever farming is not feasible: in the patchwork of rougher, thin, and sandy soils on the lower plains, and especially in the semi-arid open plains on the south and west. In the latter area the regional boundary between West and Southwest Texas cuts directly across this ranching country, for it is based upon other economic and human factors.

Oil provides the economic difference along that boundary, and a very great one it is. Oil is produced in some quantity in nearly every county of West Texas and in such enormous quantities in several as to form almost the entire basis of many towns and some of the region's largest cities. Beginning with the Electra field near Wichita Falls in 1911 every large district of West

Texas has at some time felt the impact of major discoveries. The most recent large developments have been in the Canyon Reef area around Snyder and in the Permian Basin farther west, where Midland and Odessa, two small towns twenty miles apart, were suddenly transformed into a pair of brand-new cities with 150,000 people. Almost solely the product of oil (the first being the main center for company offices and finance, the second for refining and related industries), these cities are but the most recent and remarkable exhibits of what has happened on a smaller scale to many a hamlet and ranch town in the region.

However, despite the widespread effects of oil upon economic and social conditions, it has not significantly altered the basic culture, for West Texas as a whole has remained one of the most strongly native areas of the state, created and sustained by migrations out of North, Central, and East Texas. Negroes have been a very minor, and to a considerable extent controlled, part of these migrations, meeting strong resistance except where needed for cheap labor. Today they make up 5 to 10 percent of the population of about half the counties in a distribution which very largely reflects cotton production. Until recently, except for the southern ranching fringe West Texas had very few Hispanos, but new demands for labor have brought in such considerable numbers that they are now 10 to 20 percent of the population in areas of intensive agriculture on the High Plains and its forelands. These minorities live on the edges of or in small enclaves within the towns and cities of the region, and so far they have been so few in number, so largely confined to agricultural labor, and so completely unorganized, as to have been the cause of relatively little social tension in these otherwise very homogeneous settlements.

Aside from these minorities, the population of the region is perhaps the purest example of the "native white Anglo-Saxon Protestant" culture in Texas. And it is such in the popular mind as well as in historical fact; a recent local writer on religion noted that the leaders of the largest church in his city took great pride in the fact that the South Plains was settled by a "pure blooded, homogeneous population . . . from the great Anglo-

Saxon centers of the South." Although its roots reach back into the Southern backwoods, the society is here a wholly modern one of middle-class farmers, ranchers, business and professional men, with very considerable local wealth from cotton, cattle, and oil. Emancipated from the narrowest folk expressions of Southern fundamentalism, it remains thoroughly within and indeed gives much leadership to the mainstream of Southern Protestant development, with Baptists and Methodists dominant, and the Disciples of Christ, the Church of Christ, and various other evangelical sects prominent. This general religious tradition still very directly influences reading, radio, education, forms of recreation, and social habits (the repeal of prohibition has been soundly defeated three times since 1946 in the region's largest city). The undiluted Southern background has made it a routinely segregationist society. In the past the Ku Klux Klan found strong support and in various localities there have been attempts to keep Negroes out or to drive away those few who have drifted in. Yet it is now a modern and prosperous society, sufficiently attuned to national religious, social, and political trends to produce leaders of a different persuasion and to give considerable support to basic changes in local policies and habits. Because the proportion of Negroes is everywhere quite small, at least the mechanics of official desegregation were relatively promptly and easily applied.

On the whole West Texas is a strongly conservative political area, with a form of conservatism which very directly reflects the more general history and character of the region, for that political emphasis is a fusion of the old and the new and of local and national patterns, a combination and blending of the provincial, rural, folk conservatism of the native Texan-Southern tradition with the strongly ideological economic conservatism of the newer wealthy class of the Southwest and West. Put in 1964 terms, it was a region with many Goldwater Democrats.

Abilene, on the border of the woodlands and the plains, is the self-styled capital of the region, the home of the West Texas Chamber of Commerce and other regional organizations, and of three large denominational colleges, (Baptist, Methodist, and Church of Christ) which are good expressions of and important centers for the main religious traditions of the area. But in fact Abilene is not the largest nor in many ways the principal city and it must share its role with several others, each the focus of a large trade area: Wichita Falls to the north, San Angelo to the south, Big Spring to the west, and Lubbock, the obvious capital of the Southern High Plains. A local historian has recently noted that while this last city is in many ways like any other in America,

. . . yet there is the mark of West Texas upon her. . . . she still maintains much of the spirit of small town individualism, together with a rather straitlaced moral attitude more characteristic of much smaller communities. A certain suspicion of such attributes of a modern industrial nation as government bureaucracy, labor unions, and commitments to foreign nations is to be noted. And there is also an informality of dress and habit not always found in older communities. Politics have been dominated by a group of prominent men who have stamped the city with the mark of their ideas and concepts and have forestalled the rise of a class of professional politicians.

He could have written the same of any of the other cities, for he has expressed some important traits common to the region as a whole.

G. THE PANHANDLE

Some of the differences between this West Texas and the Panhandle are obvious, others more subtle; but together they clearly indicate the latter to be a separate culture area. This high wheatland is one of the few areas of Texas beyond the historic and ecological limits of cotton and it has thus lain beyond the spread of any significant number of Negroes or Hispanos. Less obvious but certainly important, the Panhandle is the only area of Texas which does not have strong Southern antecedents. Texans came into the area, but Middle Westerners came in larger numbers and have given the dominant imprint. Thus although it is as strongly Protestant as West Texas, the expression is more that of Midwestern Protestantism, with many Baptist churches having Northern rather than Southern affiliations and with Methodism, the leading sect of so much of the American

Midlands, the largest church in several counties. And political conservatism is here rooted in the traditional agrarian Republican conservatism of Kansas and northwest Oklahoma rather than the rural Southern Democratic conservatism of the areas just to the southeast. It seems probable that the gradation in the relative strength of the Republican Party, decreasing from the northeast to the southwest corner of the Panhandle, is a rather close reflection of the proportionate distribution of Midwestern and Texan backgrounds among the population.

Panhandle communities, farm towns, oil towns, and Amarillo as well, therefore, have a homogeneity and a political and social outlook which makes them more like those of Kansas than those in other Texas regions, and such an emphasis is strongly reinforced by patterns of trade and traffic which tend to move the region's products and people more to Kansas City and the East than to Fort Worth and the Gulf.

The Texas Panhandle is therefore a markedly ambivalent region. People of older Texas ancestry are here, and the power of the Texas name, of citizenship, and of a myriad of other ties is certainly important, yet powerful influences also orient the region and bind it to the Middle West. It is difficult to measure the relative significance of these two but it is clear that the region as a whole constitutes a border zone of Texas society.

H. North Texas

In this circuit of regions a North Texas seems an obvious and necessary link between East Texas and West. In some cultural features it is clearly a transition area between the two, but altogether its identity as a culture region remains rather vague. It is an area of prosperous farms of cotton, grains, and livestock on rich blackland prairies, many thriving small industrial cities, the whole strongly dominated by the metropolitan influence of Dallas. It is very largely an Anglo area, with less variety than areas to the south, fewer Negroes than East Texas and more than West Texas. The presence of cotton here and its disappearance from East Texas reverses an original contrast between the two regions and underlies others, such as the absence of a great underemployed rural population such as is found in East Texas.

Yet there is certainly no sharp boundary between the two, and the rapid industrialization of the whole northeast is steadily blurring all distinctions. On the opposite side the virtual absence of Negroes in the Western Cross Timbers, a pattern reflecting the much lessened agricultural intensity in that particular area, provides an important contrast in a whole cluster of social features between North Texas and that particular portion of West Texas, but in other ways the two regions are much less distinct. To the south there are no sharp boundaries in any feature, and North Texas grades into Central Texas where proportions of non-Anglos begin to assume greater significance.

I. CENTRAL TEXAS

Central Texas has persisted as the great area of diversity. In this varied physical arena of woods and prairies, hills and plains, rich river bottoms and thin-soiled cuestas, there is more human variety than anywhere else in Texas: Anglos of every background, Negroes, Hispanos, and all of the European groups. Proportions and distinctions have changed over the years (the Hispanos are more important and widespread today than ever before, for example, while differences between Anglos and Europeans have certainly faded) but all the historic elements remain discernible. Local patterns vary. In some districts there are discrete clusters of different peoples: perhaps a small clannish Polish village of farmers and shopkeepers focused upon a St. Stanislaus church; nearby a larger more prosperous German community divided into Lutheran, Methodist, and Catholic congregations; and a few miles away perhaps an old Southern hamlet, half Anglo and half Negro, all Baptist, segregated and interdependent. In other areas, and especially in the larger towns and small cities such variety is brought together. The churches most obviously mirror this diversity, and a recent survey of membership in Brenham, seat of Washington County in the old Austin Colony area of the Brazos Valley, is representative:

Lutheran 1,417
Baptist (Negro congregation) 1,005
Roman Catholic 800

Methodist (white congregation)	608
Baptist (white congregation)	366
Methodist Episcopal (Negro)	185
Episcopal	150
Christian	90
Methodist (Negro)	80
Presbyterian	65
Church of Christ	48
Assembly of God	40
Jewish	40

Such proportions are unique to Central Texas and they have important social consequences. The variety alone precludes the kind of powerful uniform influence so apparent in East and West Texas for among these denominations there are very different outlooks on such matters as private and public schools, marriage and divorce, dances and drink. Central Texas is not simply part of the Bible Belt of Southern fundamentalism, nor of the Hispano-Catholic borderlands, nor is it an ethno-religious enclave—it combines important elements of all three. Similarly in politics the region is notable for providing important support for a wide range of traditions and ideologies: classic Southern conservative Democratic, liberal Democratic of Populist and New Deal leanings, traditional moderate German Republicanism, and modern right-wing ideological Republicanism. So, too, there is an unusual economic diversity. Agriculture, industry, and oil are all present and rather well balanced. Oil is now produced in only modest amounts and has not imposed its character upon new cities and whole districts; agriculture combines cotton, grains, and livestock and is not dominated by any one. Clearly the larger communities in such a region must have a social heterogeneity and consequent flexibility quite unlike anything to be found anywhere else in Texas.

Chapter VI

★ CHARACTERIZATION

~~~~~~

CENTRAL TEXAS IS APPROPRIATE GROUND ON WHICH TO SHIFT
our concern from this inventory of regional parts to some relationships among them and once again to an examination of the
whole.

A. GRADATIONS OF EMPIRE

In a way, Central Texas seems central in type as well as in
position, for a comparison of elements makes each of its bordering regions seem a kind of local specialization of some part of
its diversity—as if each had concentrated on that particular pattern of culture it was best suited to nurture. Put in more dynamic terms, these regional patterns might suggest that Central
Texas was either a source from which its various elements have
spread outward in regionally different combinations, or a focus
which has received all the various provincial patterns and combined them into a richer cultural complex. In fact, as this
lengthy essay should have made clear, such interpretations are
misleading as to what actually happened (Map 16). But even
though these patterns cannot be explained in simple environ-
mentalist or diffusionist terms, such views do contain important
elements of truth. Furthermore, if we shift our perspective
somewhat and begin to look at how these regions are actually
connected to one another we may well begin to think of a Central Texas defined not so much by its internal cultural character

as by the great cities near its corners. If we see it as a great triangle whose sides are the trafficways uniting the metropolitan areas of its three points, the functional centrality of this region to all the others is greatly magnified and illuminated. Although such a triangle is discordant in detail with the boundaries of Central Texas as a culture area, it does embrace the main body of that area and these great cities include among them the whole range of its characteristic variety. Furthermore, each of these cities is the focus of more than one peripheral region and it is through them that the parts of Texas are articulated with one another. To the extent that Texas has a region central in function and character this triangle is surely it.

We may, for the moment, therefore, take this triangle to be the Core area of Texas in the usual sense of that term: the seat of political and economic power, the focus of circulation, the area of most concentrated development and most characteristic culture patterns (Map 17). The rest of Texas is bound to that Core through the mediating functions of Houston, San Antonio, and Dallas-Fort Worth. Each of these is the great market and supply center and the great gathering place for all the various peoples of its tangential regions. Thus Houston brings East Texas and the Gulf Coast into conjunction with this Core; San Antonio provides the link with South Texas, much of the Southwest, and the German Hill Country; while Dallas and Fort Worth together bring East, North, and West into focus. We may usefully label this immediate periphery of regions as the Primary Domain of Texas—that is, an area thoroughly dominated by Texas characteristics and focused upon this Core, but with less intensity of development than the Core and with special regional variations in cultural patterns as have already been noted. All of this domain lies within the political bounds of Texas except for that outer margin of West Texas which overlaps into New Mexico. But that area is so thoroughly Texan in origins and orientations that it is in fact as much a part of the main Texas culture area as the popular local terms for the region—"Little Texas"—and its people—"Texicans"—would suggest. The recentness of this colonization and the very strong community of interests with Lubbock and Midland-Odessa far

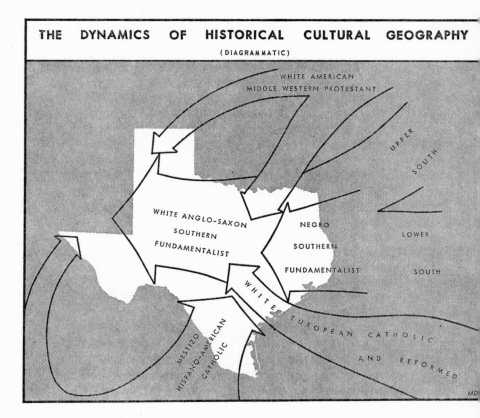

THE DYNAMICS OF HISTORICAL CULTURAL GEOGRAPHY
(DIAGRAMMATIC)

WHITE AMERICAN
MIDDLE WESTERN PROTESTANT

UPPER SOUTH

WHITE ANGLO-SAXON
SOUTHERN
FUNDAMENTALIST

NEGRO
SOUTHERN
FUNDAMENTALIST

LOWER SOUTH

WHITE EUROPEAN CATHOLIC AND REFORMED

MESTIZO HISPANO-AMERICAN CATHOLIC

Map 16

outweigh the pull of Albuquerque and Santa Fe and the political divisiveness of the border.

Extending this perspective further, the Panhandle and the El Paso district seem to be another gradation outward from the Core, a kind of Secondary Domain, firmly part of the political area and thus bound by many ties and inevitably reflecting many features common to all of Texas, yet less "Texan" in a general sense than other regions of the state, the people of the one area being very largely of a different background, and both areas being strongly oriented to non-Texan regions. Still farther beyond, a fourth category can be applied to some fringes to the east, north, and west of these Domains. Entirely in other states, these may be thought of as a Sphere of Texas Influence, wherein Texas people or Texas trade orientations are evident but Texas culture is nowhere dominant. In the southeast, Lake Charles is in function an extension of the Houston-Beaumont industrial area and in culture has more in common with those cities than with adjacent areas of Louisiana, although a Cajun element in its population and history is important. In the northeast, the Red River borderlands of Arkansas and Oklahoma are drawn into the trade areas of Paris and Texarkana. Most of the people on either side of the boundaries are of the same background and the local commercial links with Texas are further magnified by the power of Dallas. Much of southwestern Oklahoma was colonized by Texans and it is also similar in landscape and economy to neighboring areas in Texas. But except for districts near Wichita Falls, commerce is strongly bound to Oklahoma City and the Middle West. A Texan attempt to capture the trade of this borderland is still evident in the long railway line (now a branch of the MK&T) built by Wichita Falls interests. It was eventually extended almost to the end of the Panhandle and it did bring some Oklahoma wheat to Texas mills, but it is crossed or tapped at eight points by other railroad lines leading to Oklahoma and Kansas centers and thus only diverted a very small part of the total trade to Texas. The Panhandle of Oklahoma, like that of Texas, was settled by Midwesterners, but since the development of modern highways it has been drawn to some degree into the trade area of Amarillo.

The Texan influence is somewhat greater in northeast New Mexico and especially in the Pecos Valley. Texans were prominent in the early settlement and the development of trade. The first railroad into the Pecos Valley was a feeder from the Texas & Pacific; other Texas lines tapped this eastern side of New Mexico well before it had any such connections with Albuquerque, and important ties with Texas trade centers have been maintained ever since.

Even beyond this Sphere there are some scattered but important features of Texan influence, especially in farther parts of New Mexico. In some areas there are little clusters of Texans living in discrete communities, such as those so intensively studied by social scientists in the Ramah area or in the several new irrigated cotton districts in the arid valleys of the southwestern corner of the state—in each case, a tiny enclave of West Texans obviously and self-consciously aware of being different from their neighbors, still linked by occasional visits to kinfolk and friends in their former Texas homes. More common are the very considerable number of Texans within the towns and cities. Even after such people have become quite detached from their Texan antecedents they may quite unself-consciously and despite little obvious cohesion, constitute in effect a social and political bloc quite different in outlook from their Anglo neighbors. Such influences are reinforced in some districts by Texan control of important ranches, mercantile chains, banks, newspapers, and broadcasting stations. Some of this control is long-standing, much of it is a quite recent expression of Texan affluence, as is the strong penetration of Texan money into the recreational resources of Colorado, where a variety of resorts have been established and where large ranches have sometimes been purchased more for their trout streams and deer than for their cattle pastures.

We may thus complete this schematic geographic representation of Texan influence by adding this Zone of Penetration. It is quite impossible to define such an area precisely because the agents of influence are varied and difficult to assess. It does not, of course, include all areas of major Texan investment (that might include much of the world), but only those areas where-

in the financial influence reinforces such other influences of
Texan people and products as the religious revival programs on
Texan-controlled radio stations, or the political stance of certain Texan-controlled newspapers. Nor does this zone include all
the areas of Texan emigration, but only those wherein such
migrants have remained a rather obviously separate group.
Many more thousands of Texans have moved into California
than into New Mexico, but in the former they are only a small
part of a much larger influx from all parts of the nation and
soon lose any clear identity as a group, whereas a much smaller
movement may make them the dominant influence in some New
Mexican town.

Given the general pattern of expansion of Texas and the nation it was inevitable that New Mexico would become the main
area of "foreign" penetration. The firm outreach of Texas began
with the cattlemen, was consolidated by railroad builders, and
has been recurrently reinforced ever since by surges of migration and investment, as in the drought years of the 1930's, the
war years of the 1940's, and in the recent period of strong economic growth in the whole Southwest. Once the two areas became states in the same Union, there could be no legal barrier to
such movements and therefore only expansions from other
source regions could keep Texans from taking over. The indig-
enous Hispano-Indian peoples of the upper Rio Grande simply
did not have sufficient demographic and economic power to occupy and maintain firm control over the whole territory although they did spread out, rather thinly, over a wide area.
In many places they yielded ground to the invading Tejanos,
but they held on especially well in those districts better suited to
sheep than to cattle. More effective competition came from the
Anglos of New Mexico, originally Easterners and Midwesterners who have been infiltrating into the area ever since the opening of the Santa Fe Trail from Missouri, and who took the lead
in developing the territory's land and mines, railroads and commerce. Texan expansion westward therefore was countered by
the Hispano-Indian and Anglo expansion eastward out of the
upper Rio Grande and thus the Texan impress upon New Mexico weakens westward by discernible gradations: firmly domi-

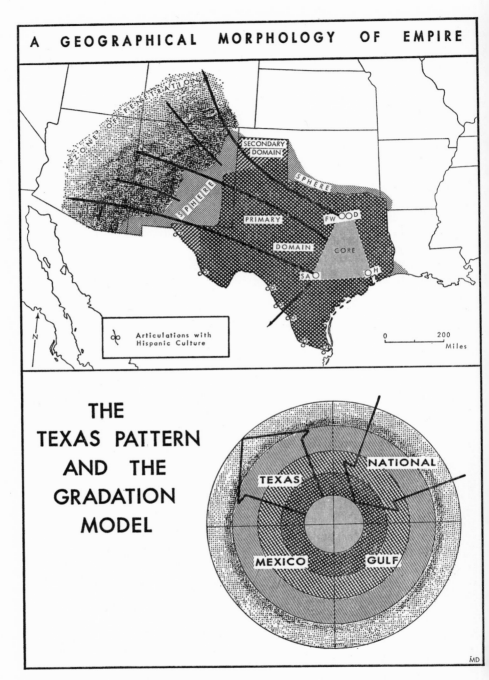

A GEOGRAPHICAL MORPHOLOGY OF EMPIRE

Articulations with
Hispanic Culture

0   200
         Miles

THE
TEXAS PATTERN
AND THE
GRADATION
MODEL

Map 17

nant on the Llano Estacado, important throughout the Pecos Valley, influential but more sporadic over much of the remainder. Certainly a steadily mounting Texan political influence is apparent, strongly affecting the stance of the local Democratic Party and assiduously lobbying in Santa Fe for the protection and furtherance of Texan investments. Indeed, "Dallas and Houston may become symbols" of New Mexico's "colonial status," a New Mexican writer recently observed, and "politicians may some day be able to win elections by inveighing against the encroachment of Texas imperialism." Thus, while Texans have not taken over the state, the imperial dreams of Texas Republic days have at least to some extent been accomplished by the mundane movements of Texan ranchers, farmers, merchants, bankers, and oilmen.

We may, then, appropriately view the five categories of Core, Primary Domain, Secondary Domain, Sphere, and Zone of Penetration as a diagrammatic summary of some important gradations in the geography of the Texas empire (Map 17). The imperial presence has been defined in terms of a combination of culture and commerce, of particular kinds of people with functional ties in particular directions. The schematic pattern so expressed is a common one of gradations, a progressive lessening in quantity or intensity, outward from a center. Matched against the full model in its simplest form—a series of concentric circles—this Texas empire fits very largely into the northwest quadrant (Map 17). The reasons for its exclusion from most of the southern quadrants are obvious, although it may be worth noting that neither the Gulf nor Mexico were inevitable barriers, for it is conceivable, for example, that filibusters or other interventions might have led to the implantation of Texas colonies in Mexico, Yucatan, or Cuba, which might have maintained important connections with their source. More importantly, we should note that while Mexico was a bar to expansion it has been an important source of immigration and cultural influences which have been essential to the vitality of the Hispano element in the Texan population. The series of twin cities spaced along the Rio Grande of course provide the immediate articulation of these Mexican-American components of Hispano

culture but they are also brought into focus in San Antonio at
the corner of the Texas Core. The weakness of the imperial pattern in the northeast quadrant reflects the historical trend of
American westward expansion and the geographical pattern of
American economic power. That quadrant has been the main
source of Texan people and of the cultural and commercial competition which for just about a hundred years has steadily undermined the reality and threatened the very idea of a Texas
empire.

B. DISPERSAL OF FOCUS

The principal impact of these powerful cultural and commercial influences from out of the northeast has been brought most
directly to bear upon the nearest point of the Texas Core. That
Dallas is the best known city of Texas, even though it is
not the largest (Houston), the most historically famous (San
Antonio), or the seat of government (Austin), is perhaps largely
an expression of its position at the threshold, the gateway between Texas and the nation. It has served as such continuously
since the arrival of the first railroads out of the north. With its
commercial importance thus established, the later federal highway system was gradually brought into focus there with a dozen
radial routes, and the city is now similarly the main node within Texas of the new interstate system of superhighways. A
clearer indication of its mediating function is provided by the
pattern of scheduled air service, for Dallas has far more flights to
more places within Texas and to more cities outside the state than
any other Texas center (Map 18). Houston, larger and richer, is
a poor second. Although Dallas is primarily a regional focus and
a link between Texas and the nation, it is also of course an inter-
mediate point within larger patterns, between California and
the Southeast, Chicago and Mexico, for example: a crossroads
in an ever-thickening national and international web—and,
again, much more so than any other Texas city. Viewed against
both its historical background and this national position, it is no
paradox that this most famous of Texas cities is the least "Texan" in cultural character.

The volume of air service suggests that the strongest pulse of

Texas life throbs along the arteries connecting its three great urban systems. Similar maps of other kinds of communication would only further emphasize the importance of this triangle, and the way the rest of Texas is bound to it. But we must now admit that such patterns do not fit the common generic concept of a core area. In the usual model of such a spatial system, power, density, and concentration are greatest at a central point, and in the most common empirical examples a single great city serves as the political capital, financial center, commercial focus, seat of learning, and religious headquarters. A core area is therefore most commonly a nuclear region dominated by such a node and is more obviously defined by its center than by its periphery. Clearly in Texas these attributes are distributed among several centers rather than concentrated on one. Because of the special terms of annexation the state government has greater legal powers than those of any other state, yet Austin is a relatively weak focus. It is of little commercial importance, it never became the crossroads its founders envisioned, it has today for example little direct air service to the several regions of the state. And even though it is the seat of the principal university, higher education in Texas is widely dispersed and is to an unusual degree shared among leading religious denominations and the state; the leading institutions are in this Core, but dispersed among Fort Worth, Dallas, Waco, Houston, College Station, and Austin.

Such a core therefore seems rather hollow and it does not appear likely to be filled either by a concentration of much greater power and development in Austin, or by the continued spread and eventual coalescence of its corner cities into a single vast interconnected Texan megalopolis. Even though this triangle is only a small part of Texas, it is 200-250 or more miles on a side. It is conceivable that because of their central position Temple, Hearne, and Bryan could become the area of greatest attraction and growth and form a nexus binding together all these peripheral urban systems, but certainly the scale of things is far too great for this to be an immediate prospect. While we may reaffirm our original statement that insofar as Texas has a core this triangle is certainly it, we must also add that the

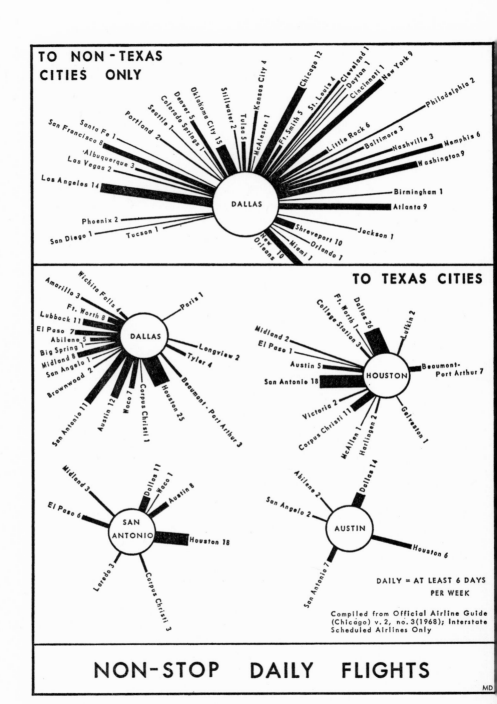

TO NON-TEXAS CITIES ONLY

Santa Fe 1 · San Francisco 8 · Portland 2 · Seattle 1 · Colorado Springs 1 · Denver 5 · Oklahoma City 15 · Stillwater 2 · Tulsa 5 · Kansas City 4 · McAlester 1 · Ft. Smith 5 · Chicago 12 · St. Louis 4 · Cleveland 1 · Dayton 1 · Cincinnati 1 · New York 9 · Philadelphia 2 · Little Rock 6 · Baltimore 3 · Nashville 3 · Memphis 6 · Washington 9 · Albuquerque 3 · Las Vegas 2 · Los Angeles 14 · Phoenix 2 · San Diego 1 · Tucson 1 · New Orleans 10 · Miami 1 · Orlando 1 · Shreveport 10 · Jackson 1 · Birmingham 1 · Atlanta 9 · DALLAS

TO TEXAS CITIES

DALLAS — Amarillo 3 · Wichita Falls 4 · Ft. Worth 8 · Lubbock 11 · El Paso 7 · Abilene 5 · Big Spring 2 · Midland 8 · San Angelo 1 · Brownwood 2 · San Antonio 11 · Austin 12 · Waco 7 · Corpus Christi 1 · Houston 25 · Beaumont - Port Arthur 3 · Tyler 4 · Longview 2 · Paris 1

HOUSTON — Midland 2 · El Paso 1 · Austin 5 · San Antonio 18 · College Station 3 · Ft. Worth 2 · Dallas 26 · Lufkin 2 · Beaumont - Port Arthur 7 · Galveston 1 · Harlingen 2 · McAllen 1 · Corpus Christi 11 · Victoria 2

SAN ANTONIO — Midland 3 · El Paso 6 · Dallas 11 · Waco 1 · Austin 8 · Houston 18 · Corpus Christi 3 · Laredo 3

AUSTIN — Abilene 2 · San Angelo 2 · Dallas 14 · Houston 6 · San Antonio 7

DAILY = AT LEAST 6 DAYS PER WEEK

Compiled from Official Airline Guide (Chicago) v. 2, no. 3 (1968); Interstate Scheduled Airlines Only

NON-STOP DAILY FLIGHTS

MD

Map 18

very character of that triangle reveals how far Texas is from being a simple, single, centrally focused entity.

Of course it never was. The dispersal of central functions began when Houston, the most promising commercial center, failed to become the primary political center. With the arrival of the railroads from the north, central commercial functions also became dispersed among more cities and a strong rivalry between divergent orientations was firmly established. Such historical competitions are still discernible within the networks of today but they defy any simple differentiation for they vary according to mediums, products, seasons, and rates. Furthermore, Texas, like any other large part of the United States, is a group of regions loosely articulated through a few great cities and bound by a myriad of ties to the rest of the nation, and so dense and complex is the over-all circulatory system that today a Gulf orientation can hardly be viewed as any more "Texan" and less "national" than any other. In this sense, Texas has been not only integrated but rather thoroughly assimilated into the nation.

C. VARIETIES OF CULTURE

If, as a final exercise, we examine this triangle as a Core which is central in type of culture as well as the focus of various functions we encounter further, and rather analogous, complications. For just as Texas lacks a single great city as a primary nucleus and focus, so it is impossible to identify a single elemental culture pattern to which all the various local expressions of culture are basically tied. Just as its central functions are dispersed among several cities, so culture is expressed in at least four different basic patterns. Of the many peoples who have contributed to the life of Texas the most important of those which have maintained the clearest cultural identity are the Anglos of Southern tradition, the Catholics of strong European heritage, the Hispanos, and the Negroes. As our survey has already shown, each of these is found in greatest dominance in some adjacent region (West Texas, the Hill Country, South Texas, East Texas, respectively), but all four are important in Central Texas. In the broad patterns of historical movement

Central Texas has been the principal zone wherein all of the
lesser groups have converged upon the dominant westward-mov-
ing Southern Anglos. Therefore, just as the great cities of the
Core are closely interconnected and the life of Texas is very
much bound up with the traffic between them, so in this Core
(and to varying extents in these same cities) these several
peoples live in closest physical contact and the full array of patterned social relationships between them is exhibited. And, to
push the analogy still further, despite this geographical convergence and the resulting juxtapositions, a merging and blending
of these several cultures into a single new Texas culture is even
more remote than the coalescence of the several cities into a
single new megalopolis, for the social distances are even greater
than the geographical.

The Typical Texan of popular lore and the Texas culture of
sociological description are of course stereotypes of the Texas
Anglo of Southern heritage and thus less generally applicable
to the population of Central Texas than to several other Texas
regions. Here such Anglos share the area with Negroes, Hispanos, and German Catholics, to name only the most obvious
among the variety, and thus to summarize the culture of Central Texas we would need similar characterizations of at least
these other three. It is not a case of each being entirely different
from the others in every important particular, but of each
being critically different in at least a few fundamentals. Theo-
retically one might postulate an ultimate absorption of all the
others into the generally dominant Texas Anglo culture, or the
integration and ultimate blending of all four into a distinctively
new Texas culture, or various partial developments of such possibilities. But although these peoples already share a number of
traits and some pairs share a great many, and although further
cultural convergence is bound to take place, there is simply little
to suggest that, in the near future, assimilation or acculturation
will remove to any important degree the really fundamental differences. One might postulate that the Typical Texan of some
future time will be a brown-skinned, bilingual, Evangelical
Catholic, whose values and patterns of life exhibit a happy har-
mony of individual freedom and the social good, but it would be

an idle exercise which only a non-Texan, far removed from the exacerbating problems of daily life where any two of these people share a community, might suggest, and he need only look around him wherever he may be in America to see that there is precious little evidence anywhere that such might be the likely results of acculturation. None of this discussion is meant in any way to be prescriptive, to define those directions of cultural change which are more desirable than others; the point is that one can neither simply add up these peoples as they are and talk about *a* Texas culture nor reasonably anticipate any significant lessening of the differences among them in the near future. In Southern Baptist and Roman Catholic, Anglo-American and Hispano-American, Southern White and Southern Negro, we are dealing with three of the strongest polarities in American society. While no one of these is peculiar to Texas, only in Central Texas are all three brought together in such magnitude. Furthermore, these barriers and antagonisms not only co-exist in the same region but complicate and reinforce one another, as, for example, in the somewhat stronger racial and religious components in the Anglo-Hispano problems of Texas than in the relations of the two in some other states.

Central Texas, therefore, is not a Core in the sense of being the central region of or exhibiting the purest or highest form of the particular culture most characteristic of the whole, but only in the sense that it best displays together the several cultures which have been most important in the heritage of Texas and thereby also best displays the full range of intercultural tensions which are so important a part of Texas life. Certainly it is here, especially in the major cities, that cultural change will take place most rapidly, not only because of the freer more flexible patterns of urban life but because in such cultural relations, as in commerce, it is through these centers in this region that the pressures and influences of national policies and practices are brought most directly to bear upon Texas society. And in these matters as in other patterns of change Texas seems to be thoroughly part of the nation, showing little autonomy or initiative, but being shaped like all the rest by federal laws and broad educational trends, mass communications and population mobility, economic affluence and corporation networks, a broadening world outlook and a deepening social consciousness, into an increasingly cohesive and uniform national pattern. Despite some twentieth-century updating the image of the Typical Texan seems destined to require further revisions which will make him increasingly more like the Typical American.

Nevertheless, three important kinds of patterns yet remain to distinguish Texas from the nation: the serious insistence by the majority of Texans on thinking of themselves as different, on proclaiming boldly an allegiance to Texas as well as to the United States; the residue of certain values and related social attitudes and behavior which sociologists have identified as especially (though not uniquely) characteristic of the main body of the Texas population; and the particular regional patterning of peoples, a distinctive Texan mosaic, related in its parts to, but not duplicated as a whole in, any other part of the country.

Thus if we conclude that it is a gross oversimplification to call Texas a region, a culture, or an empire, we must nevertheless also conclude that Texas is something more than just one-fourteenth of the American area, one-twentieth of the American people, and one-fiftieth of the American union. To whatever degree it may have been in times past in some sense "an empire in itself" it is obvious that now it is increasingly captive within the strands and relentlessly under the influence of a very much larger and more powerful cultural and political unit—and yet it is just as obvious that it will long persist as a distinctive piece in the fabric of the American nation.

SOURCES

I did not wish to clutter the text of this essay with notes and references, but I do wish to make quite clear to anyone interested the materials I have used in its preparation.

I have grouped these according to the most appropriate sections and where feasible I have made further groupings with reference to main topics. There is often, of course, a considerable overlapping, but except for a few cases where a work was as important in one section as another I have avoided duplicate listings. At the end of the list for each section I have identified the source of each direct quotation. Abbreviations are used as follows:

QTSHA—*Quarterly of the Texas State Historical Association*;
SWHQ—*Southwestern Historical Quarterly*.

The following works were important throughout: Rupert Norval Richardson, *Texas: The Lone Star State* (Englewood Cliffs, New Jersey: Prentice-Hall, Inc., 1958); Stanley A. Arbingast and Lorrin Kennamer, *Atlas of Texas* (Austin: Bureau of Business Research, University of Texas, 1963); *Texas: A Guide to the Lone Star State*, American Guide Series, Federal Writers Project, (New York: Books, Inc., 1940); and, especially, the *Texas Almanac*, published more or less regularly, first in Galveston, later in Dallas, since 1857. I have used various volumes of this last, a veritable cornucopia of information about Texas, from the first to the latest; and I am convinced that the very existence, perpetuation, content, and tone of this remarkable compendium is one of the best evidences of the personality and individuality of Texas.

The major types of material used which do not appear in this list are maps and atlases and census reports. As I wrote each section I had maps contemporary to that era before me and I made quick surveys of many others. These are an indispensable tool for such geographical interpretation, but as most of them are not readily available in libraries I do not believe that a long list would be of much help to the reader. Excellent bibliographies of the map collections of various Texas libraries are available. In addition to the routine United States census reports, I found the series of maps of Texas showing population distribution at each census in Jeanne Johnston Grimes, "One Hundred Years of Population Expansion in Texas, 1850–1950," unpublished masters thesis, Southern Methodist University, 1953, and the series showing decennial population changes by county, 1850–1960 in Sven Dahl, "Hur Texas Befolkats," *Meddelanden Från Handelshögskolans I Göteborg Geografiska Institution N:o 76*, 1962, to be especially helpful.

Finally, I would like to emphasize that the materials listed for the last two sections were less important in total than the impressions gained from a series of rapid but carefully planned field reconnaissances, from the quick perusal of an array of contemporary maps, newspapers, directories, journals, and other materials, and from discussions with various Texas friends.

I. Implantation

General Sources

Herbert Eugene Bolton. *Texas in the Middle Eighteenth Century.* Berkeley: University of California Press, 1915.

Robert Carleton Clark. *The Beginnings of Texas 1684–1718.* Bulletin of the University of Texas No. 98, Humanistic Series No. 6. Austin: The University of Texas, 1907.

Odie B. Faulk. *The Last Years of Spanish Texas, 1778–1821.* The Hague: Mouton & Co., 1964.

Samuel Harman Lowrie. *Culture Conflict in Texas, 1821–1835.* Columbia University Studies in History, Economics and Public Law, No. 376. New York: Columbia University, 1932.

On Colonization

Mattie Austin Hatcher. *The Opening of Texas to Foreign Settlement, 1801–1821.* University of Texas Bulletin No. 2714, April 8, 1927. Austin: The University of Texas, 1927.

Mary Virginia Henderson. "Minor Empresario Contracts for the Colonization of Texas, 1825–1834," *SWHQ*, 31 (April, 1928), 295–324; 32 (July, 1928), 1–28.

William H. Oberste. *Texas Irish Empresarios and Their Colonies.* Austin: Von Boeckmann-Jones Company, 1953.

Ethel Zivley Rather. "DeWitt's Colony," *QTSHA*, 8 (October, 1904), 95–191, with 4 maps.

Rex Wallace Strickland. "Anglo-American Activities in Northeast Texas, 1803–1845." Unpublished Ph.D. dissertation, The University of Texas, 1937.

Contemporary Descriptions

Juan N. Almonte. "Statistical Report on Texas," translated by Carlos E. Castañeda, *SWHQ*, 28 (January, 1925), 177–221.

"Descriptions of Texas by Stephen F. Austin," *SWHQ*, 28 (October, 1924), 98–121.

José María Sánchez. "A Trip to Texas in 1828," translated by Carlos E. Castañeda, *SWHQ*, 29 (April, 1926), 249–288.

Other

Mattie Alice Austin. "The Municipal Government of San Fernando de Bexar, 1730–1800," *QTSHA*, 8 (April, 1905), 277–352.

I. J. Cox. "The Southwest Boundary of Texas," *QTSHA*, 6 (October, 1902), 81–102.

Malcolm D. McLean. "Tenoxtitlan: Dream Capital of Texas," *SWHQ*, 70 (July, 1966), 23–43.

W. S. Red. *The Texas Colonists and Religion, 1821–1836.* Austin: E. L. Shettles, 1924.

Quotations

p. 34, comments of the Nacogdoches land commissioner: Richardson, p. 82.

p. 36, comments on San Felipe: Sánchez, p. 271, and Almonte, p. 199, respectively.

II. Assertion

General Sources

William Ransom Hogan. *The Texas Republic: A Social and Economic History.* Norman: University of Oklahoma Press, 1946.

Stanley Siegel. *A Political History of the Texas Republic 1836–1845.* Austin: University of Texas Press, 1956.

H. Yoakum. *History of Texas from Its First Settlement in 1685 to Its Annexation to the United States in 1846.* 2 vols. New York: J. S. Redfield, 1855.

Imperial Framework

Charles A. Bacarisse. "Why Moses Austin Came to Texas," *Southwestern Social Science Quarterly,* 40 (June, 1959), 16–27.

William Campbell Binkley. *The Expansionist Movement in Texas 1836–1850.* Berkeley: University of California Press, 1925.

Ethel Zivley Rather. (trans.) "Explanation to the Public Concerning the Affairs of Texas, by Citizen Stephen F. Austin," *QTSHA,* 8 (January, 1905), 232–258.

J. W. Williams. "The National Road of the Republic of Texas," *SWHQ,* 47(January, 1944), 207–224.

Ernest William Winkler. "The Seat of Government of Texas," *QTSHA,* 10 (October, 1906), 140–171; (January, 1907), 185–245.

Migration and Colonization

E. Bagby Atwood. *The Regional Vocabulary of Texas.* Austin: University of Texas Press, 1962.

Terry G. Jordan. "The Imprint of the Upper and Lower South on Mid-Nineteenth-Century Texas," *Annals of the Association of American Geographers,* 57 (December, 1967), 667–690.

Barnes F. Lathrop. "Migration into East Texas 1835–1860," *SWHQ,* 52 (July, 1948), 1–31; (October, 1948), 184–208; (January, 1949), 325–348.

William Wilson White. "Migration into West Texas, 1845–1860." Unpublished M.A. thesis, The University of Texas, 1948.

Regions and Cities

Gilbert Giddings Benjamin. *The Germans in Texas: A Study in Immigration.* Philadelphia: University of Pennsylvania, 1909.

Mary Margaret Bierman. "A History of Victoria, Texas, 1824–1900." Unpublished M.A. thesis, The University of Texas, 1948.

Rudolph Leopold Biesele. *The History of the German Settlements in Texas, 1831–1861.* Austin: Von Boeckmann-Jones, 1930.

Seymour V. Connor. "A Statistical Review of the Settlement of the Peters Colony," *SWHQ,* 57 (July, 1953), 38–64.

George L. Crockett. "East Texas in the Politics of the Republic," in Eugene C. Barker (ed.), *Readings in Texas History*, pp. 394–404. Dallas: Southwest Press, 1929.

George C. Engerrand. *The So-Called Wends of Germany and Their Colonies in Texas and in Australia.* The University of Texas Bulletin No. 3417. Austin: The University of Texas, 1934.

Earl Wesley Fornell. *The Galveston Era: The Texas Crescent on the Eve of Secession.* Austin: University of Texas Press, 1961.

Dorothy Kelly Gibson. "Social Life in San Antonio, 1855–1860." Unpublished M.A. thesis, The University of Texas, 1937.

William J. Hammond and Margaret F. Hammond. *La Réunion: A French Settlement in Texas.* Dallas: Royal Publishing Co., 1958.

Houston: A History and Guide. American Guide Series. Houston: The Anson Jones Press, 1942.

Terry G. Jordan. *German Seed in Texas Soil: Immigrant Farmers in Nineteenth-Century Texas.* Austin: University of Texas Press, 1966.

Henry R. Maresh. "The Czechs in Texas," *SWHQ*, 50 (October, 1946), 236–240.

Christine Judy Mehan. "Polish Migration to and Settlement in the United States: A Geographical Interpretation." Unpublished M.A. thesis, Syracuse University, 1965.

Joseph Milton Nance. *After San Jacinto: The Texas-Mexican Frontier, 1836–1841.* Austin: University of Texas Press, 1963.

Ermance V. Rejebian. "La Reunion: The French Colony in Dallas County," *SWHQ*, 43 (April, 1940) 472–478.

Dorothy Waties Remick. "The City of Kent," *SWHQ*, 29 (July, 1925), 51–65.

Rupert Norval Richardson. *The Frontier of Northwest Texas 1846 to 1876.* Glendale, California: Arthur H. Clark Co., 1963.

George H. Santerre. *White Cliffs of Dallas: The Story of La Reunion, The Old French Colony.* Dallas: The Book Craft, 1955.

Frank H. Smyrl. "Unionism in Texas, 1856–1861," *SWHQ*, 68 (October, 1964) 172–195.

Mollie Emma Stasney, "The Czechs in Texas." Unpublished M.A. thesis, The University of Texas, 1938.

Paul Schuster Taylor. *An American-Mexican Frontier: Nueces County, Texas.* Chapel Hill: University of North Carolina Press, 1934.

Lyder L. Unstead. "Norwegian Migration to Texas: A Historic Resume with Four 'America Letters'," *SWHQ*, 43 (October, 1939), 176–195.

Julia Nott Waugh. *Castro-Ville and Henry Castro Empresario.* San Antonio: Standard Printing, 1934.

Joseph McConnell Weston. "Social Cleavages in Texas: A Study of the Proposed Division of the State," *Columbia University Studies in History, Economics and Public Law,* Vol. 119, No. 2. New York: Columbia University, 1925.

Seb. S. Wilcox. "Laredo during the Texas Republic," *SWHQ*, 42 October, 1938), 83–107.

Contemporary Accounts

John Russell Bartlett. *Personal Narrative of Explorations and Incidents in Texas, New Mexico, California, Sonora, and Chihuahua,* 2 vols. Chicago: The Rio Grande Press, Inc., 1965.

Mary Austin Holley. *Texas.* Lexington, Kentucky: J. Clarke & Co., 1836.

Frederick Law Olmsted. *A Journey through Texas.* New York: Mason Brothers, 1859.

Dr. Ferdinand Roemer. *Texas: With Particular Reference to German Immigration and the Physical Appearance of the Country.* Translated by Oswald Mueller. San Antonio: Standard Printing Co., 1913.

C. F. Schmidt. "Victor Friedrich Bracht: A Texas Pioneer," *SWHQ*, 35 (April, 1932), 279–289.

Other

"A Group of Theses on *The Architecture and Culture of Early Texas,*" by students in Course 350 A, July, 1942, University of Texas, (mimeographed). Barker Library, The University of Texas, Austin.

Ernest Allen Connally. "Architecture at the End of the South: Central Texas," *Journal of the Society of Architectural Historians,* 11 (December, 1952), 8–11.

Dubose Murphy. "Early Days of the Protestant Episcopal Church in Texas," *SWHQ*, 34 (April, 1931), 293–316.

Charles J. Potts. *Railroad Transportation in Texas.* Bulletin of the University of Texas No. 119, Humanistic Series, No. 7. Austin: The University of Texas, 1909.

Robert Schick. "Wagons to Chihuahua," *The American West,* 3 (Summer, 1966), 72–79.

Quotations

p. 38, all quotes on the Texas Republic: Walker (see Section IV),
   p. 17.
p. 40, Austin on Santa Fe trade: Rather, p. 235.
p. 42, on location of capital: Winkler, pp. 217–220.
p. 43, on routes of migration: Lathrop, p. 201.
p. 46, on terms for physical regions: Holley, p. 23.
p. 47, on East and West Texas: Olmsted, pp. 418–419.
p. 53, on Gonzales: Olmsted, p. 237.
p. 58, on San Antonio: Olmsted, pp. 148–150.
p. 61, on coastal route: Olmsted, p. 365.

III. EXPANSION

General Sources

William Curry Holden. *Alkali Trails: Or Social and Economic Movements of the Texas Frontier, 1846–1900*. Dallas: Southwest Press, 1930.
Homer Lee Kerr, "Migration into Texas, 1865–1880." Unpublished Ph.D. dissertation, The University of Texas, 1953.
Richardson. *The Frontier of Northwest Texas* (see Section II).
John S. Spratt. *The Road to Spindletop: Economic Change in Texas, 1875–1901*. Dallas: Southern Methodist University Press, 1955.

Networks and Commerce

Bernard Axelrod. "Galveston: Denver's Deep-Water Port," *SWHQ*, 70 (October, 1966), 217-228.
James Marshall. *Santa Fe: The Railroad That Built an Empire*. New York: Random House, 1945.
V. V. Masterson. *The Katy Railroad and the Last Frontier*. Norman: University of Oklahoma Press, 1952.
Richard C. Overton. *Gulf to Rockies: The Heritage of the Fort Worth and Denver-Colorado and Southern Railways, 1861–1898*. Austin: University of Texas Press, 1953.
Potts. *Railroad Transportation in Texas* (see Section II).
S. G. Reed. *A History of the Texas Railroads and of Transportation Conditions under Spain and Mexico and the Republic and the State*. Houston: St. Clair Publishing Co., 1941.
William F. Switzler. "Report on the Internal Commerce of the United States for the Fiscal Year 1889," *House Executive Documents No. 6, Part 2*, 51st Congress, 1st Session, 1889–1890.

Harry Williams, Jr. "The Development of a Market Economy in Texas: The Establishment of the Railway Network, 1836–1890." Unpublished Ph.D. dissertation, The University of Texas, 1957.

Other

Della Tyler Key. *In the Cattle Country: History of Potter County.* Amarillo: Tyler-Berkley Co., 1961.

Graham Landrum. *An Illustrated History of Grayson County, Texas.* Fort Worth: University Supply & Equipment Co., 1960.

J. W. Petty, Jr. (ed). *Victor Rose's History of Victoria.* Victoria: Book Mart, 1961.

The Prairie's Yield: Forces Shaping Dallas Architecture from 1840 to 1962. New York: Reinhold Publishing Co., 1962.

F. Stanley, *Rodeo Town (Canadian, Texas).* Denver: The World Press, 1953.

M. F. Sweetser. *King's Handbook of the United States.* Buffalo: Moses King Corp., 1891.

Robert H. Talbert. *Cowtown-Metropolis: Case Study of a City's Growth and Structure.* Fort Worth: Texas Christian University, 1956.

Nathanial Alston Taylor. *The Coming Empire: Or Two Thousand Miles in Texas on Horseback.* Revised edition. Houston: N. T. Carlisle, 1936.

George A. Wallis. *Cattle Kings of the Staked Plains.* Dallas: American Guild Press, 1957.

Quotations

p. 74, on trade through Topolobampo: *The New York Times*, Sunday, June 11, 1967.

p. 74, on Houston's imperial position: Sweetser, p. 823.

p. 75, on Sherman and Denison: Landrum, p. 29.

p. 75, Jay Gould on Dallas: *The Prairie's Yield*, p. 17.

p. 77, on lumber industry: Easton (see Section IV), p. 95.

p. 77, on the economy of Texas: Caldwell (see Section IV), p. 405.

p. 77, on Texas individuality: Benedict and Lomax (see Section IV), pp. 57–58.

IV. ELABORATION

General

Francis McNeill Alsup. "A History of the Panhandle of Texas."

Unpublished M.A. thesis, University of Southern California, 1943.

E. C. Barksdale. *The Meat Packers Come to Texas.* Texas Industry Series No. 7, Bureau of Business Research. Austin: The University of Texas, 1959.

Edwin L. Caldwell. "Highlights of the Development of Manufacturing in Texas 1900–1960," *SWHQ*, 68 (April, 1965), 405–431.

Hamilton Pratt Easton. "The History of the Texas Lumber Industry." Unpublished Ph.D. dissertation, The University of Texas, 1947.

Lawrence L. Graves (ed.). *A History of Lubbock.* Lubbock: West Texas Museum Association, 1962.

Henry S. Shryock, Jr. *Population Mobility Within the United States.* Chicago: University of Chicago, 1964.

Texas Almanac, various recent volumes on the historical sequence of oil discoveries and the history of production.

Typical Texan

John Bainbridge. *The Superamericans.* Garden City: Doubleday & Company, 1961.

Joseph Leach. *The Typical Texan: Biography of an American Myth.* Dallas: Southern Methodist University Press, 1952.

Michael McGiffert. *The Character of Americans: A Book of Readings.* Homewood, Illinois: Dorsey Press, Inc., 1964; especially selections by Robin M. Williams, John Gillin, and Cora Du Bois.

Emma Jean Walker. "The Contemporary Texan: An Examination of Major Additions to the Mythical Texan in the Twentieth Century." Unpublished Ph.D. dissertation, The University of Texas, 1966.

Evon Z. Vogt. "American Subcultural Continua as Exemplified by the Mormons and Texans," *American Anthropologist,* 57 (1955), 1163–1172.

————. *Modern Homesteaders: The Life of a Twentieth-Century Frontier Community.* Cambridge: Harvard University Press, 1955.

Other

H. Y. Benedict and John A. Lomax. *The Book of Texas.* Garden City: Doubleday, Page & Company, 1916.

Joseph Kelly Johnson. "Borger: A Study of Community and Personal Disorganization in a Texas Oil Town." Unpublished M.A. thesis, The University of Texas, 1930.

V AND VI. DIFFERENTIATION AND CHARACTERIZATION

General

Warren A. Beck. *New Mexico: A History of Four Centuries.* Norman: University of Oklahoma Press, 1962.

Harley L. Browning and S. Dale McLemore. *A Statistical Profile of the Spanish-Surname Population of Texas.* Population Series, No. 1, Bureau of Business Research. Austin: The University of Texas, 1964.

Dellos Urban Buckner. "Study of the Lower Rio Grande Valley as a Culture Area." Unpublished M.A. thesis, The University of Texas, 1929.

Robert J. Casey. *The Texas Border and Some Borderliners: A Chronicle and a Guide.* Indianapolis: Bobbs-Merrill Co., 1950.

Ross Calvin. *Sky Determines: An Interpretation of the Southwest.* Revised and enlarged. Albuquerque: University of New Mexico Press, 1965.

R. L. Chambers. "New Mexico: Land of Disenchantment," *Frontier: Voice of the New West*, 1 (January, 1950).

Churches and Church Membership in the United States: An Enumeration and Analysis by Counties, States and Regions. New York: National Council of Churches of Christ in the U.S.A., 1956–1958.

Commercial Atlas and Marketing Guide. Chicago: Rand McNally and Company, 1966.

Agnes Brown Cummins. "The Physical and Cultural Geography of Parts of San Patricio and Aransas Counties, Texas." Unpublished M.A. thesis, The University of Texas, 1953.

C. R. Draper and Daniel Russell. *Rural Organization in Val Verde County, Texas.* Miscellaneous Publication Number 71 (March, 1951). College Station, Texas: Texas Agricultural Experiment Station, 1951.

Marvin Ray Felder. "The Politics of the Texas Gulf Coast, 1945–1960." Unpublished M.A. thesis, The University of Texas, 1960.

Erna Fergusson. *New Mexico: A Pageant of Three Peoples.* New York: Alfred A. Knopf, Inc., 1951.

Edwin Scott Gaustad. *Historical Atlas of Religion in America.* New York: Harper & Row, 1962.

Govita Gonzalez. "America Invades the Border Towns," *The Southwest Review*, 15 (1930), 469–477.

Werner F. Grunbaum, "Desegregation in Texas: Voting and Action Patterns," *Public Opinion Quarterly*, 28 (1964), 604–614.

David Hamilton. "Imperial Texas and Its Satellite States," *Frontier: The Voice of the New West*, 10 (August, 1959), 9–10.

Max Sylvius Handman. "The Mexican Immigrant in Texas," *Southwestern Political and Social Science Quarterly*, 7 (June, 1926), 33–41.

Robert A. Hasskarl, Jr. *Brenham, Texas 1844–1958*. Brenham: Banner-Press Publishing Co., 1958.

Pauline R. Kibbe. *Latin Americans in Texas*. Albuquerque: University of New Mexico Press, 1946.

Oscar Lewis. *On the Edge of the Black Waxy: A Cultural Survey of Bell County, Texas*. Washington University Studies—New Series, Social and Philosophical Sciences, No. 7. St. Louis: Washington University, 1948.

William Madsen. *The Mexican-Americans of South Texas*. New York: Holt, Rinehart & Winston, 1964.

J. W. Millard. *Atlas of Wholesale Grocery Territories*. Domestic Commerce Series, No. 7, Bureau of Foreign and Domestic Commerce, Department of Commerce. Washington, D.C.: U.S. Government Printing Office, 1927.

Green Peyton. *The Face of Texas*. New York: Thomas Y. Crowell, 1961.

Edward T. Price. "The Central Courthouse Square in the American County Seat," *The Geographical Review*, 58 (January, 1968), 29–60.

Arthur J. Rubel. *Across the Tracks: Mexican Americans in a Texas City*. Austin: University of Texas Press, 1965.

Ozzie G. Simmons. "Anglo Americans and Mexican Americans in South Texas: A Study in Dominant-Subordinate Group Relations." Unpublished Ph.D. dissertation, Harvard University, 1952.

James R. Soukup, Clifton McClesky, and Harry Holloway. *Party and Factional Division in Texas*. Austin: University of Texas Press, 1964.

Fred Anderson Tarpley. "A Word Atlas of Northeast Texas." Unpublished Ph.D. dissertation, Louisiana State University, 1960.

Paul Schuster Taylor, *An American-Mexican Frontier* (see Section II).

John Edward Weems. "A Gateway of a Gaining Nation: Nacogdoches, Texas," in Thomas C. Wheeler (ed.), *A Vanishing Amer-*

ica: The Life and Times of the Small Town. New York: Holt, Rinehart & Winston, 1964.

Logan Wilson. "A Sociological Study of Huntsville, Texas." Unpublished M.A. thesis, The University of Texas, 1927.

Nathaniel Wollman. "The Southwest in the Nation: Some Interregional Relations," in David Revzan and Ernest A. Engelbert (eds.), *Interregional Linkages,* Proceedings of the Western Committee on Regional Economic Analysis of the Social Science Research Council. Berkeley: University of California, 1954.

Sister Frances Jerome Woods. *Mexican Ethnic Leadership in San Antonio, Texas.* The Catholic University of America Studies in Sociology, vol. 31. Washington, D.C.: 1949.

Joseph L. Zarefsky. "Spanish Americans in Houston and Harris County" (Mimeographed). Houston: Research Bureau, Community Council, 1953.

Wilbur Zelinsky. "An Approach to the Religious Geography of the United States: Patterns of Church Membership in 1952," *Annals of the Association of American Geographers,* 51 (June, 1961), 139–193.

Quotations

pp. 104–105, on population of West Texas: Graves, p. 473.

p. 106, on Lubbock: Graves, p. viii–ix.

p. 117, on Texas imperialism in New Mexico: Hamilton, p. 10.

INDEX

Abilene, Texas: 105–106

Alabama: as source of people, 29, 43, 47, 50; migration routes from, 43

Alamita, Texas: 55

Alamo, the: 37, 58

Albuquerque, New Mexico: Texans' seizure of, 42

Alsatians: in Castro colony, 45, 51

Amarillo, Texas: as focus of Middle Western and Texas competition, 76–77, 107, 113; as capital of Panhandle, 83; and Kansas, 107; and Oklahoma, 113

Anahuac, Texas: 32

Anglo-Americans. SEE Anglos

Anglos: definition of, 8; as Mexican colonists, 31, 32, 33; and Germans, 53, 103; in San Antonio, 58; and cattle industry, 66–69; into Rio Grande Valley, 83; and "Typical Texan" image, 86, 90, 122–123; in East Texas, 92, 94; in South Texas, 99–101; in Southwest Texas, 101–102; in West Texas, 104–105; in North Texas, 107; in Central Texas, 108; summary of role of, 121–123

Apache Indians: 69

Arizona: railroad line across, 71

Arkansas: as source of people, 29, 34, 48, 64, 96; Northeast Texas as a country of, 34; migration routes from, 43; Texas influence in, 113

Atascosa River: 84

Atchison, Topeka & Santa Fe railroad: 76

Austin, Texas: selection of, as capital, 42; attempts to remove capital from, 46–47; as relatively weak focus, 119

Austin, Moses: 28

Austin, Stephen F.: 28–30, 35, 40

Austin Colony: 28–31, 50, 51

Bahia, La, Texas: 55. SEE ALSO Goliad, Texas

Baytown, Texas: 96

Beaumont, Texas: 79, 80, 95, 96

Beaumont-Houston area: as focus of oil industry, 80; unity of culture in, 113

Beeville, Texas: 55

Bexar, Department of: description of, 32–33; Hispanos expelled from, 46

Blackland Prairies: of North Texas, 48; as sources of settlers, 64; as focus of railroads, 72

Midlands. SEE Middle West

Midwest. SEE Middle West

missions: in Spanish Texas, 24, 26

Mississippi: migration route from, 43

Missouri: as source of people, 29, 48, 64; migration route from, 43; railroad line through, 72

Missouri, Kansas & Texas Railway: 72, 74, 113

Mobeetie, Texas: 76

Monclova, Mexico: as governmental seat for Texas, 26

Moravia: as source of people, 65

Moravians: in Central Texas, 52

Mormons: in Texas Hill Country, 52

Nacogdoches, Texas: as early Spanish center, 24–25; as portal to Texas, 27, 31, 43; as Mexican fort, 32; in 1834, 33; Catholics in, 94

Nacogdoches, Department of: 32; in 1834, 33–35

Nacogdoches region: regional consciousness of, 46

Navasota River: 43

Neches River: settlers along, 34, 43

Negroes: definition of, as term, 9; in Central Texas, 51, 108; in North Texas, 69, 107–108; proportion of, in population, 85; place of, in social hierarchy, 89, 90; in East Texas, 92, 94, 95; in Gulf Coast region, 97; in German Hill Country, 103; in West Texas, 104, 105

New Braunfels, Texas: German nucleus in, 51–52; Olmstead's description, 53–54

New England: as source of people, 57

New Mexico: Texas interest in, 39, 40; railroad links with, 64, 71, 72, 76; and Texas cattle industry, 68, 69; extension of Texas people and patterns into, 76–77, 80, 82, 112–117

New Orleans, Louisiana: on migra-

tion routes, 43; East Texas in contact with, 47; Galveston link to, 57; railroad links, 61, 72

New Ulm, Texas: 51

New York: as source of people, 57; Galveston link to, 57

North, the: defined as region, 9; as source of people, 83, 85, 96

North Texas: in 1860, 48–50; lack of city in, 59; contrasts with East Texas, 64; Missouri slaveowners flee to, 64–65; and cattle industry, 68, 69; as focus of trafficways, 72; impact of railroads on, 74–75; as a modern region, 107–108; as part of Primary Domain, 111

Norwegian colony: in Central Texas, 52

Nueces River: as a boundary, 23; Irish colony on, 31; as limit of Texas Republic control, 39; brigandry beyond, 65; and cattle industry, 66, 68; agriculture along, 84. SEE ALSO South Texas; Trans-Nueces country

Nuevo Santandar, Mexico: founding of settlements in, 24; Texas as a shield for, 27

Odessa, Texas: 104. SEE ALSO Midland-Odessa area

Ohio Valley: migration route from, 43

Oklahoma: tapped by Texas railroads, 64; Texas claims and infiltrations in, 76; as source of people, 96; areas in Texas Sphere, 113

oil industry: character and impact of, 79–81; influence of, upon popular attitudes, 88; in East Texas, 94; impact of, upon Gulf Coast, 95–96; in West Texas, 103–104; in Central Texas, 109

Oldenburg, Texas: 51

Orange, Texas: 95